T0194476

DEAR DAUGHTER

 also by

HEATHER ARMSTRONG

It Sucked and Then I Cried

DEAR
DAUGHTER

The Best of the Dear Leta Letters

HEATHER ARMSTRONG

creator of dooce.com

G

GALLERY BOOKS

New York   London   Toronto   Sydney   New Delhi

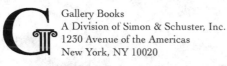

Gallery Books
A Division of Simon & Schuster, Inc.
1230 Avenue of the Americas
New York, NY 10020

First Gallery Books hardcover edition April 2012

GALLERY BOOKS and colophon are registered trademarks of
Simon & Schuster, Inc.

For information about special discounts for bulk purchases,
please contact Simon & Schuster Special Sales at 1-866-506-1949 or
business@simonandschuster.com.

The Simon & Schuster Speakers Bureau can bring authors to your
live event. For more information or to book an event contact the
Simon & Schuster Speakers Bureau at 1-866-248-3049 or visit our website at
www.simonspeakers.com.

Designed by Jaime Putorti

Manufactured in the United States of America

10 9 8 7 6 5 4 3 2 1

Library of Congress Cataloging-in-Publication Data

Armstrong, Heather B.
  Dear daughter : the best of the dear Leta letters / Heather Armstrong.— 1st ed.
    p. cm.
1. Mothers and daughters. I. Title.
  HQ755.85.A758 2012
  306.874'3--dc23

                         2011051353

ISBN 978-1-5011-0916-4
ISBN 978-1-4516-6142-2 (ebook)

For my mother, Linda

MONTH TWO

Dear Leta,

Tomorrow you are officially eight weeks old. I am sitting here typing this as you lie sleeping next to me. Over the weekend, your father and I discovered that if we place you on your stomach you will actually sleep longer than five minutes at a time. Every modern medical journal will tell you never to let your baby sleep on her stomach, but with the blessing of your pediatrician, who let all of his own kids sleep on their stomachs, we decided to give it a try. When you have your own kids they will probably have a pediatrician with a very different opinion. Listen to her. Also, don't tell on us.

This morning, in fact, I had to wake you up after three whole hours of sleeping soundly on your stomach, and when I rolled you over you had the cutest case of Binky Face, all mushed and covered in binky-shaped indentations.

I wish they made Binky Face bread tins so that I could bake a loaf of banana bread in the shape of your

sleeping profile, and then instead of trying to eat your chubby cheeks I could just eat the banana bread. That would probably be better for both of us.

Yesterday I read in one of the dozens of medical books we bought since your birth that babies your age can sometimes wrap their fingers around objects that are held close to their hands. Your father and I ran and got the rattle that your uncle Shan and aunt Sydney gave you and held it close to your right hand, and you wrapped your fingers around that thing so hard it almost snapped in two. And then, proving once again that you probably have ancestors from the planet Krypton, you began waving that rattle around like you were flagging down a plane.

Your father and I got so excited and we started cheering, "GO BABY GO!" At that moment I totally forgave you for the hours and hours and did I mention hours? of sleep I have lost getting out of bed at night to walk into your room to put the binky back in your mouth.

You totally snorted in your sleep just now. A gigantic snort, and remarkably it didn't wake you up. For the past couple of weeks when you have been attempting sleep on your back you have been waking yourself up by smacking yourself in the face repeatedly. There have been nights when I've brought you back to bed with me that you have punched me in the nose with your little clenched fist and I've had to walk around the next day with a swollen nostril.

We've tried swaddling you, and in the first month of your life swaddling totally worked and you looked like a little frog-caterpillar hybrid. But your arms have become strong enough in the past month that you can break free of any of our swaddles, your father's swaddles included, and your father could swaddle a full-grown octopus and it wouldn't be able to wiggle its arms.

A side effect of your Flailing Infant Arm Syndrome is your discovery of your right hand, which you like to chew on at every possible opportunity. Your hand chewing is very drooly, dripping with drool, and if I don't keep up with the drool the entire right side of your face becomes slimy with drool bubbles, which you don't seem to mind at all.

I look forward to this next month with you, to more coos and noises and near giggles, to more of the moments like the other night when I was feeding you at one thirty and you kicked your sleeping father in the head. Your father and I love you more than you could possibly know, and you won't know or understand just how much until you have a child of your own.

Love,
Mama

MONTH THREE

Dear Leta,

This week you turn three months old. We put you to bed every night sometime between six and eight o'clock, depending on how you've slept during the day, and we always go through the same ritual of bathing you, dressing you, and feeding you. This ritual is our favorite part of the day, and one night last week your father was late coming home from work and I had to bathe you by myself. I have never seen your father so devastated! He missed bath time with his little Thumper, a nickname we've given you because whenever we lay you down on the changing table you immediately begin thumping it with both your legs so violently that the whole changing table shakes.

You LOVE the changing table. You love it more than the swing or the bouncy seat, and sometimes you love it more than being held by me or your father, and we promise not to hold that against you.

During the night you will usually sleep in stretches that last anywhere from three to five hours, and you will also go right back to sleep after you eat. When you wake up in the morning at about seven you are always smiling, and Leta, those morning smiles are the reason your father and I decided to have kids. Your smile is brighter than the sun, the most beautiful addition to my life.

For the past five days, you have slept well both at night and during the day and you have only screamed ONCE, and that was yesterday when I tried to put you in the BabyBjörn, the contraption that holds you to my chest so that I can walk with my hands free. I couldn't figure out how the straps worked, and you were being very patient, and then somehow I flipped you upside-down and the strap wrapped itself around your face, and I would scream, too, if my mother mushed my nose between two metal snaps.

We love you, little Thumper.

Love,
Mama

Dear Leta,

Tomorrow you turn four months old. I have been trying to keep up with all the changes going on in your life, but even in the last twenty-four hours you've learned something new, and I can only type so fast. This is one of those moments when I wish I could TiVo you, press Pause, and replay you over and over again so that I don't miss anything.

A couple of days ago, you learned how to blow bubbles and make tugboat noises with your tongue. This was an inevitable development as you were trying to figure out what to do with all that drool. Where did you learn to drool like that? We could water the lawn for a month with all the drool that seeps out of your mouth on a daily basis. Perhaps all this drool is compensation for the fact that you never spit up, ever, except for that one time we were outside talking to the neighbors and you hurled all over your father's new black business shirt, right after we had just proudly announced, "She never spits up!"

You've discovered both your hands, and they are the most marvelous creations you have ever seen. You suck on your fingers and then your fist and sometimes we look over and you have both your thumbs in your mouth, as if one thumb just isn't enough. When we're dressing you for bed at night and we have to pull your pajamas over your arms, you are separated from your hands for all of three seconds, and the look of panic on your face seems to say that you are worried that you will never see them again, O wonderful hands, where have ye gone? And then you are reunited with them, your long-lost friends, and you get so excited that you almost hyperventilate, sticking both fists into your mouth so violently that you almost choke on your knuckles.

This month you also discovered the joy of sticking things into your mouth. One night a few weeks ago, you were lying on your back on our bed and I dangled a teething ring over your head. The room got very quiet, and time seemed to shift into slow motion as you reached up, grabbed the teething ring, opened your mouth, and tried to bring the teething ring to your tongue. But you missed your tongue. You missed your whole mouth altogether and tried to stick the teething ring into your ear. You did this three consecutive times, shoving the teething ring into your ear, and then into your forehead, once into your nose, and then, as the Mormon Tabernacle Choir swelled to a triumphant, room-shaking Hallelujah! you brought the teething ring to your mouth! Fireworks exploded in the distance as you took the teething ring out of your mouth and then put it back in, over and over again, as if putting that thing in your mouth was what you were born to do. As you squealed in celebration I said good-bye to my old life and hello to my new one, a life that will be consumed with running to grab potentially harmful things out of your hands before they make it to the inside of your eager, drooling mouth.

You are becoming such a little person, and every day I have to resist the urge to put you between two slices of wheat bread and slather mayonnaise on your head, gobbling you up in one bite. Things are so much more fun now that you have graduated into an actual baby, one that I can play with, one who responds to my voice and my touch. Your giggles and squeals are delightful, and the once intolerable screaming has been replaced with occasionally hilarious fussiness, thunderous squawks of displeasure as you try to communicate with me that you are mad or angry or just so tired of it all! I've never seen a baby so exasperated, and now I have to resist laughing at you because you sound like a really angry bird.

I know you're awake when I hear you scratching the mattress. It's your way of letting me know that it's time to come get you, SCRATCH SCRATCH SCRATCH. I can hear the scratching from the most remote point in the house, even outside in the backyard. It's not the prettiest sound, and it makes my spine twitch every time I hear it, but it also breaks my heart it's so damn cute. It's also cute when your father is holding you in the BabyBjörn and you scratch his arm like you scratch the mattress, and then you grab hold of his arm hair and yank it like you're pulling weeds. He shrieks a bit from the sting, but that is okay, because that's his way of sharing in the pain since he didn't have to birth you or suffer engorged, torpedo boobs.

What a great month, little one. Just when I think my love for you couldn't be any bigger, I wake up and discover that I love you even more, and I worry that my body isn't big enough to hold this much love. I worry that my insides may explode because there isn't any more room.

Love,
Mama

Dear Leta,

Today you turn five months old. Five! Whole! Months! You're practically an adult! Isn't it about time you started paying rent?

The first thing we should talk about is how you've slept through the night five nights in a row. And when I say slept through the night, I don't mean six or seven hours in a row. Six or seven hours is for three-month-olds, for *babies*. When I say slept through the night, I mean twelve hours in a row.

You have discovered the joy of sleeping, something you definitely inherited from me. Your naps are now all an hour or longer, sometimes even two hours. And when we put you in the crib for a nap you smile, bring your fist to your mouth, and close your eyes. When you wake up in the morning, you usually lie in the crib for five to ten minutes just playing with your blankets and examining your hands, waiting for us to come get you. And when we come get you it's like you're playing the slots and have just hit JACKPOT! Your whole body convulses with excitement and you gasp and smile and squint your forehead with glee! The look on your face seems to say THERE IS THAT WOMAN WHO FEEDS ME! or THERE IS THAT MAN WHO MAKES ME LAUGH!

And since we're talking about the laughing . . . you have this low, back-of-the-throat laugh that sounds like a fake laugh. Sometimes it sounds like you are laughing to make us feel good about our attempts to make you laugh, like, "Haha, I know you're trying to be funny, but you're really not that funny, and since I don't want you to feel bad, I'll just go ahead and laugh anyway." It sounds so fake that I always expect you to roll your eyes.

But then there are the full-bodied chuckles that only your father can seem to elicit from you, and every time he makes you chuckle, openmouthed and wide-eyed, he gives you the hiccups. This wouldn't normally be a problem except that it always happens right before bedtime. So the whole time I'm feeding you dinner you're hiccupping, and the hiccups continue throughout your bedtime story. Sometimes the hiccups don't stop until about ten minutes after you've fallen asleep.

This month you have learned how to reach for things, which is rather unfortunate, because you haven't yet learned how to balance yourself, so anytime you reach for something you end up face-first on the floor or the couch. Surprisingly, this isn't nearly as frustrating as being bored, and you could remain in the face-plant position for several minutes without announcing any sort of discomfort. I don't know if that's because you trust me to come running to your rescue or because you're studying the pattern on the floor and want to be left alone in your research.

Also this month I have gone on a diet consisting of orange juice, strawberry Pop-Tarts, and your chubby cheeks. I cannot keep your face out of my mouth, it is just so scrumptious and plump and round. You have a lot more hair on your head, so instead of putting your whole head in my mouth, I bite your ears and nose and gnaw on your chin. And then I go back for more cheeks. Sometimes I just can't stop and I end up swallowing you whole, and I walk around with your feet hanging out of my mouth, and when your father comes home from work he asks, "Where's the baby?"

Love,
Mama

Dear Leta,

This month you have spent most of your waking hours grabbing things and shoving them into your mouth. There is nothing in this world off-limits to your grabbing and eating. You've gobbled other people's hair, the wireless phone antenna, ceramic drink coasters, the dog's tail, and both of your feet *at the same time*.

I'll never forget the first time you took hold of your right foot and pulled it to your mouth. You were lying on the changing table getting prepped for bed, and you snatched up that foot like you were stealing food off someone else's plate. And then you stuck it in your mouth, and the stunned look on your face seemed to say, "What is this? A third hand? To chew on? You mean I have three hands? Why have you been hiding this from me, this third hand to chew on?" I could see the cogs in your brain clicking and clacking as you suddenly realized that if there was a third hand, *there just might be a fourth one around here somewhere*! And there you were, my chubby, naked baby contorted like a pretzel on the changing table, all the limbs of your body in your mouth. You looked up at me as if to say, "This, *this* is the American dream."

This month you also took your first trip on an airplane. We had a blast in San Francisco, seeing friends and taking pictures of the architecture and riding public transportation. At a diner on Geary I fed you a couple of bites of a chocolate malt, and after each bite you would turn your head to look at me and beg for more. I promise I will always share my chocolate malt with you, if you promise to keep wrapping your arm around my neck when I scoop you out of your bed.

While we were waiting in the Salt Lake airport for our plane to arrive, I got you to fall asleep on my shoulder, for the very first time. It was no small feat, and I had to walk up and down the terminal and sing out loud, but you eventually gave in to the exhaustion and passed out in the curve of my neck. That was one of the most beautiful moments of my life, having you there motionless and heavy from sleep, the smell of your powder-fresh head smeared across my cheek.

Leta, you are so lovely. You have made my life so complex and crazy and intense, but recently I have been waking up really early and counting the minutes until you wake up. I get so excited to see those Armstrong eyes and that Hamilton chin, and I want to rush in and ask you if you want to play. I'll hold your feet while you eat them!

Love,
Mama

P.S. You rolled over today! Twice! And then immediately looked up at us like *What the heck just happened?*

Dear Leta,

Some people might say that there is nothing special about turning seven months old; you can't get your driver's license or purchase alcohol. But what they don't know is that with the seven-month mark comes the Pop-Tart and pickles privilege. What could be more special than that?

Just this morning your father and I spent over a half hour sharing our strawberry Pop-Tart with you, giving you little bites with the yummy strawberry filling. You gummed the pieces with sheer delight, making *mmmm, mmmm* noises and waving your hands. Several times you tried to grab the Pop-Tart out of my hand, but oh no, little Scooter. I didn't want strawberry Pop-Tart all over the walls or stuck in my hair or flung through the window into the driveway. You've got quite an arm on you.

You're barely big enough to see over the tray in the high chair, but you're pretty good at reaching your hands up and grabbing handfuls of Cheerios. Gobs and gobs you grab, and you bring a fistful of O's to your mouth, but that's where you become stumped, like, I've got them close to my mouth, NOW WHAT DO I DO? Some of them make it to your chin, others to your ears, but most of them end up on the floor and in Chuck's mouth. That was a lottery win for Chuck, billions and billions of treats on the floor. Your relationship with Chuck is remarkable. He loves to lick your face after you've been fed a bottle, and you sit there with your nose scrunched up and your eyes closed in a state of half bliss and half bewilderment. Who is this beast that lives in your house? This beast with fur and fangs and wiry whiskers that tickle when he sniffs your face? Whenever he enters the room, you stare at him in amazement and then giggle for no reason other than the fact that this creature exists. Chuck is happy to amuse you, you who have come into this house and disrupted his peaceful life as the only child, you who consume most of Mama's attention.

A few days ago, just as you were waking up from your first morning nap, I walked into your room and your smell hit me like a monsoon. That was one of the most peaceful moments of my life, being wrapped with the blanket of your fragrance, knowing that I would get to spend the whole day with you. When I picked you up out of the crib you looked at me and smiled, your trademark gummy smile, and this look of recognition flashed across your face that said, "Hey! It's YOU!"

You have been utterly joyous these past few days. You are constantly smiling and giggling, laughing out loud with your whole body. And the noises that come out of your mouth span the whole alphabet. Your father and I just sit and stare at you, amazed that such an extraordinary being sprouted from the two of us. You are my sweet Zing Zing Zing Bah, my Punkin Head Piggy.

I love you,
Mama

Dear Leta,

Yesterday you turned eight months old. We have several things to talk about, but the first and most important things that we need to discuss are the two teeth that have taken up residence in your mouth and in our house. I had no idea what two teeth could do to a human being, and the world will never be the same. There is no wrath on earth as vengeful as the wrath of a teething baby, and I challenge anyone to stick their hand anywhere near your mouth without pulling it back missing a finger or five.

Over the past month, you have learned how to sit up by yourself. It happened overnight, like BOOM, there you were sitting there hanging out without tilting or leaning over. You're constantly reaching for things and grabbing the remote or telephone out of my hands. You inspect objects like a scientist, end over end, and then you try to put things into your mouth from every angle. First the top of the thing goes into your mouth, then the bottom, and then the sides. One new object can entertain you for almost a half hour, but if you've already seen something you cannot be bothered with it. You've already seen that bunny! You've already played with that rattle! And this Tupperware container? You saw it TWICE yesterday. You get this really frustrated look on your face that says, "PEOPLE! CAN'T YOU BE MORE ORIGINAL? How big is this world that you brought me into, and these are the toys that you bring me?!"

You're now eating three meals a day in addition to the bottles we feed you. You love oatmeal and pears and sweet potatoes and apples and cereal, and last week we fed you pulled pork. You'll eat just about anything we feed you, and when we put food into our mouths we had better be prepared to share that food with you as you accost us with an open mouth, like a hungry baby bird.

Over the weekend you spent two days with Grandmommy while your father and I "reconnected." I promise you will understand what that means when you have your own kids. When we walked into her house yesterday to pick you up you were sitting in the middle of her floor surrounded by cousins and toys, and both your father and I felt a rush of electricity shake us in our bones. We were SO excited to see you, our little Scooter sitting there smiling, waving your arms and wiggling your hands. We never knew we could miss something so much.

We picked you up and hugged you, and then I handed you to your father so that I could go to the bathroom really quickly, and Leta, for the first time you cried as I turned to walk away. My mother assured me that you hadn't cried all weekend, but there you were looking after me as I stepped closer to the bathroom, and gigantic tears fell from your eyes. I couldn't help myself, so I turned back around and scooped you out of your father's arms and took you to the bathroom with me. And there we were in Granny's bathroom, me on the toilet, you on my lap, smiling and peeing and being very much in love.

Love,
Mama

MONTH NINE

Dear Leta,

Today you turn nine months old. This means that you have been outside my womb for as long as you were inside it. At first it seemed you didn't like it on this side that much, but you have turned into one of the most giggly, tender, and joyous creatures that ever lived.

In the last month we have met Leta The Person. You are no longer this little blob of a thing that I take care of and wipe up but this flailing, wiggly little personality that likes certain things and really, really doesn't like other things. You love pears. You do not like peaches and will fling them at me if I try to feed them to you. You like applesauce. You do not like vanilla custard and you make this horrible gagging noise as it sits in your mouth and tries to make an innocent descent into your throat. You love to be tickled under your neck and around your thighs. You do not like it when I try to eat your nose, and you'll look at me like, "Mom, that is so not cool."

In the last week you have discovered that if you throw yourself backward while sitting on my lap, the whole world turns UPSIDE-DOWN! You LOVE to throw yourself backward and gurgle as you do it, and then you wait there for me to tickle you on your neck, and it is just the funniest thing in the whole world to you. If I'm late to tickle you on the neck you make this jerking motion with your body that seems to say, "Hey. Hey! You're supposed to tickle me on the neck now. Why are you veering from the routine? I can only stay in this thrown-back position for so long, woman!"

You are not yet mobile; you aren't crawling or scooting or rolling across the floor. You're just very content to sit there surrounded by toys, and when you see other kids walking or crawling you stare at them like, "Why are they wasting such precious energy? Do they not know that EVERYTHING can be delivered right to them? That's what this whole *baby* thing is about." Right now I'm confident that you're going to be fine developmentally, that you'll eventually want something so badly that you'll move your body in its direction somehow. But I have to admit that having you immobile is kinda convenient. I can turn my back and not worry that you'll be halfway across the room about to put your tongue into a light socket.

We finally have a solid routine during the day, one that can be timed by the clock, and you seem to like it just as much as I do. Within minutes of your naptime, you show me signs of fatigue and make it solidly clear that you want nothing more than to curl up in your crib. The biggest sign that you are tired is the rapid sucking of your thumb. Yes, the nightmare that people warned me about CAME TRUE: You are a thumb sucker! You suck your thumb, and surprisingly, THE WORLD STILL TURNS. The best part about your thumb sucking is, well, okay, there are two best parts about your thumb sucking:

1. It takes you about three or four times to get your thumb into your mouth right. You'll bring it to your mouth, and then pull it away, and then bring it close again, and then pull it away, like, "No, no, no, that's just not right!" The rest of your fingers caress your nose as you do this, and then finally, when you get your thumb into your mouth JUST RIGHT, your whole body relaxes.

2. You suck your thumb rather loudly when you sleep. So loudly that we can hear it through the monitor, and your father is constantly telling me to turn that thing down. I like to hear it, because it lets me know that you are asleep and happy and snuggly with your friend, the thumb.

I love you, Leta. I love that you hug me tightly before I put you down for naps. I love it when you growl like a bear because you know that it makes me laugh. I love how you like to turn the pages in books. I love it that you cry when I leave and then brighten up like a sun-flooded room when I come back. I will always come back to you.

Love,
Mama

Dear Leta,

There are so many good things, like how you hug me and put your nose to my nose. Like the way you smile when your father comes home from work. Like the way you kick your frog legs before the bath. Like the sound of your laugh and how it heals my heart. Like the size of your pearl-white thighs and how you'll let me gobble them up. Like how you know which button to push to turn on the TV. Like how you play with the dog's collar and he licks your face. Like the curve of your round belly and how it hangs over your pants. Like how you love books and their pages and say, "GO GO GO," as you turn them. Like how I can pick you up when you're crying and you'll put your head on my shoulder and try to get closer.

I promise to say *You are the light of my life* much more often.

Love,
Mama

MONTH ELEVEN

Dear Leta,

Today you turn eleven months old. Right now you're in your crib for your morning nap and I am sitting in the living room listening through the monitor to you talking to yourself. Before you fall asleep you also like to pat your right hand against the mattress and kick your left foot up and down. If these habits are any indication, we've given birth to the female Stewart Copeland, and if that is the case I can't wait for you to go on tour and pay for our retirement. We could live with you on your tour bus and drink a couple of beers after each show. WHO SAYS YOUR MAMA CAN'T HANG?

For the past two weeks your two top teeth have been trying to make their way into the world. Leta, those two teeth are HUGE. I didn't know babies could have such gigantic teeth. They are as big as walrus tusks. You can bite through cardboard boxes and rip holes in stuffed animals. Yesterday I gave you a sealed box of Dulcolax to entertain you for just a few seconds while I wiped down the kitchen counters. Within two seconds you had gnawed through the box and were on the verge of puncturing an actual tablet wrapped in plastic coating. I had to shove my fingers into your mouth to dig out portions of the box, and then I picked you up, set you on my hip, and called the police. "Please arrest me," I begged them.

Your first Christmas was a week ago, and your father and I decided that Santa Claus should only bring you three gifts because that's what Jesus got. Santa brought you colored blocks, some sort of pop-up toy, and the orange Boohbah. You were far more interested in the wrapping paper than the toys. We spent a few days with Grandma and Grandmommy, who both gave you clothes and toys that you immediately turned over to find the tags. It's like you've got Tag Radar, and no matter how cute or snuggly the toy, if it doesn't have a tag IT'S USELESS.

Although you probably have no idea what you're saying you have a habit of repeating "Go" on command. Sometimes you even say, "Go, dog, go," and seriously, IT IS THE CUTEST THING OH MY GOD. "Go, go, go, go, go," you'll say, and then you'll smile and clap your hands with pride. You love to play peekaboo and will continue to play it looooong after I have become bored and want to play something else, but even after the hundredth time you pull down the frog blanket to reveal your face you giggle just as heartily as if it were the first time. This month you have also developed a great love for your rubber ducky, for sticking your tongue out, for reaching out to grab my tongue, for acting shy when your father walks in the door from work, for smiling at strangers in the grocery store, for opening your mouth like a baby bird when we feed you small bites of our cinnamon rolls, for blabbing incessantly while being fed applesauce, for sucking your thumb while riding in the car.

This month I have memorized the curve of your smile, the dimples in your cheeks and forehead, the point at which the curls at the back of your head meet your neck. I am so thankful to have you here, to have your giggles echo through the house, the noise of your life in my ears, my beautiful daughter, my little LeeLee.

Love,
Mama

Dear Leta,

Happy Birthday, beautiful girl. You're a whole year old. Just think, only twenty more to go before you can buy bourbon. I've been thinking for a while about what I was going to tell you on your birthday, and I think I need to start by telling you how badly I wanted to have you. Your father and I had only been married a month when I started, ahem, threatening to go off birth control because I was ready and tired of waiting. I would never have gone off birth control without telling your father—although you are proba-bly related to hundreds of women on my side of the family who do that often—because we knew that having you was going to be a hand-in-hand effort from the beginning. We didn't have insurance at the time, and I knew that having a baby without insur-ance was not an option. So I would tell him, "You have exactly one month to find us some insurance before I go off the pill." He didn't find insurance for another eight months. You could say he took me VERY seriously.

The day that we were eligible for insurance I stopped taking the pill. That was at the beginning of April 2003, and I was sure that I would be pregnant by the end of the month. The women on my side of the family are as fertile as the day is long, something your granny might say, and Granny gave birth to ten kids. Her reproductive system knows what it is talking about. So your father and I went straight to it and pretty much did nothing but, ahem, try to make a baby for four weeks straight. That was one of the most fantastic months of my life.

On April 25, 2003, I started my period and was completely devastated. It was the first period I had experienced off the pill in over seven years, and it felt like it was going to kill me. I stayed in bed for two days with monumental cramps and cried all day long. I thought, What if I'm not like the women in my family? What if I can't get pregnant? Your father had to calm me down in one tear-filled rampage when I started babbling nonsense about how we'd have to go on fertility drugs and they wouldn't work until I was forty and then they'd all of a sudden work and I'd have quadruplets all at once and I'd never be able to care for them because I WAS SUCH A FAILURE. I apologize now for the hormones you have inherited from the Women Who Came Before You.

We decided that we'd just keep trying, and I sought the advice of my doctor. She told me specifically which days of the month I would be most likely to conceive, so I planned in advance to engage in the act of making a baby at least fourteen times during those two days, if not twenty-four or thirty-four times. Unfortunately, those two days happened to be the days that your father moved all our furniture and boxes into the house from storage, all 7,800 pounds of it. He came in from returning the moving van, totally exhausted, and I was standing in the bedroom door RARING TO GO. He looked at me like, "Heather, it would take an act of GOD right now."

The next night over dinner I collapsed into tears again and accused your father of falling out of love with me. I actually screamed at him, "I'M OVULAT-ING, AND YOU DON'T LOVE ME." I was worried that he was making excuses because he didn't want to have a baby with me, but he had just moved 7,800 pounds' worth of junk WITH HIS BARE HANDS. My ovaries could wait a few hours. I'm pretty sure you were conceived that night.

On Wednesday, May 28, three days after my period was supposed to start, I woke up at 4:30 a.m. unable to sleep and took a pregnancy test. It was positive, and I cannot adequately express in words how I felt when I saw the double pink line: joy, relief, indescribable excitement, like I was going to conquer the world. We immediately started brainstorming ideas for names and settled on "Fawnzelle La Bon Marché Armstrong" so that our families would be horrified. You just wait, one day you will RELISH the endeavor of making me uncomfortable.

Here you are now, a year after they laid you on my chest and you reached your arm out to me. Those first few weeks with you have changed me forever. They were the hardest, most terrifying weeks of my life, not because you weren't wonderful in every single way, but because I was not as confident as I thought I was going to be. I was not prepared IN ANY WAY for what having a baby would do to my life, to my heart, to my capacity for worry and love. Here I've managed to last twelve months. And you did, too! LOOK AT YOU GO. You are a totally different kid now than when we brought you home. For one, you sleep at night. I didn't think that would ever happen, and I can remember one night last March when I was certain I had given birth to the world's first human being who required no sleep.

One of the greatest things about your personality now is how coy you are. When you hear your father pull into the driveway at night you immediately try to hide in my shirt, and when he comes into the house you start laughing and peeking at him from over my shoulder. You do the same thing when you hear the dog coming into the room, or when Grandmommy comes to visit. I love how you sit and read books to yourself, and since you can't yet read, of course, the books are always upside-down and the only words you can get out are "DUCK!" or "DOG!" or "BUHBUHBUH!" even if the book is totally not about ducks or dogs or buhs, but about pigs going to market.

I also love how you grin with your nose scrunched up, your mouth full of all these teeth that are sticking out in different directions. I love how excited you get after bath time when your father holds you in front of the mirror, so excited that you almost pass out from screeching with glee, so excited that you kick your legs and have knocked your father square in the groin on more than one occasion.

Leta, I feel like I have been given a second chance at life, a life through the magic of your eyes, a life that I am finally able to appreciate fully. The world has more color in it because you are looking at it, music is a bit louder because you are hearing it. I never knew how funny a noise could be until you laughed at it, or just how excruciatingly handsome your father was until I saw your profile next to his. I thought that there was meaning in my life before you came along, but I didn't even know the meaning of meaning. For the majority of my life I thought I had religion, but never has there been a more reverent moment in my life than walking into your room late at night to watch you breathe, to hear your life in the air.

Love,
Mama

MONTH THIRTEEN

Dear Leta,

The majority of the past month has been spent watching you develop your crawling style, and I have to admit that I was a little afraid early on. Your interpretation of the crawl was an abomination of the human form, an almost painful display of two sets of uncoordinated DNA colliding. But you caught on pretty quickly and now you crawl exactly like they say you're supposed to crawl, alternating hands and knees in a forward direction. This means that you should be able to read by the time you're sixteen. Make us proud.

This month you have also figured out how to open things, things that aren't supposed to be opened, things with LOCKS HOLDING THEM SHUT. You know the unlock code on the babysitter's cell phone and once called her Peruvian boyfriend, Chimmy. Chimmy has taken hold of your heart somehow because you will say things for that boy that you won't say for anyone else, things like "Uh-oh," and "Wow wow wow," and "Taco." You can open locked drawers, cosmetic cases, every type of cell phone, and even sealed CD cases. That's the first thing you do when you encounter a new object, determine how the heck the thing opens, and even if it's not an object that opens YOU FIGURE IT OUT. Your little long fingers love to turn pages and pull at tags and pluck stray hairs on your father's neck. You know how to take Grandmommy's earrings out of her ears without drawing blood. Speaking of Grandmommy, last week you imitated her saying GRANDMOMMY, except it came out sounding like GAM MEE.

Sometimes your father will pat your back while he's hugging you and you will in turn pat his shoulder. One night you were patting his shoulder and saying, "Oglee oglee oglee," over and over again and your father looked at me and said, "Doesn't this just make your heart sing?"

Yes, yes it does, like the thumping buzz of a sub-woofer. Already I am starting to notice that you are becoming an independent creature choosing certain directions to crawl and certain toys to play with. You no longer cry when the babysitter shows up or when we leave you for a few hours with Grandmommy. In fact, you know you're about to have a good time, and I can almost see the mischievousness in your eyes. And while this thrills me, makes my heart sing bass lines and soar with pride that you are your own soul, I can't help but start to think, My God, slow down. Don't go so fast. Stay awhile.

Love,
Mama

MONTH FOURTEEN

Dear Leta,

Yesterday you turned fourteen months old. About an hour ago you figured out which button on the cordless phone activates the speakerphone. You were holding the receiver in your hand when you hit the button and this horrible dial tone roared into the room at a volume comparable to a tornado siren. It scared the holy living poop out of you. You immediately tossed the phone across the room, let out an audible "Ahhh!" and looked at me like, "You didn't tell me it was going to do THAT." And I said back to you, "Well, you can't just go around pressing buttons without expecting consequences." And I meant that on SO many levels, levels you will certainly understand once you figure out how to purposefully embarrass me in public. Despite your initial trepidation you crawled back over to where you had thrown the phone and proceeded to turn on the speakerphone, turn off the speakerphone, on, off, on, off. Yesterday was the first day of the time change, and while you normally go to bed at 7:00 p.m., by 5:30 you were already so tired that you were crawling on the floor WHILE YOU WERE SUCKING YOUR THUMB. This caused you to rest your head on the floor at the same time, so you moved around the house on both knees, a hand, and an elbow, your head a bumper. Surprisingly you don't get into too much trouble when I'm not in the room to catch you, because what's the fun in that? The fun is knowing that you're not supposed to open that drawer, and when I look at you and say, "Nu-uh-uh!" you go ahead, jerk open the drawer, and then flee the room GIGGLING. You cherish this and challenge me to follow you throughout the house so that I can SEE you doing things you know you're not supposed to do. This morning you sat at the top of the stairs and would move your hand over the landing just to hear me say, "NU-UH!" You did this repeatedly and I fell for it every time.

This month you've also learned how to sneak the dog treats underneath the tray of your high chair. I cannot believe how sneaky you are about this. You know how to distract me so that I don't see you giving all your food to the dog, who is hidden behind your dangling feet. The only reason I catch you is because you betray your ruse by laughing out loud.

Leta, I have to say, to know you is to love you, to fall head over heels in love with you. Your personality only gets more adorable every day, every minute. I love it when your father and I are talking, and to get our attention you will talk babble at a volume louder than our conversation. I love how you can give an entire monologue in one vowel, your voice rising and falling as you ask rhetorical questions and pose scenarios, "Ahhhhhh, AHHHHHH? AHHH?? Ah. Ah ah ah ahhhh ahh ahh. Ah, ah ah ah . . . AH!" I miss the days when you would pronounce your name as Leego, because now you say it exactly as it is supposed to sound, Leta. But that's okay because you say Mama a lot more now, too. You're also good at saying BYE, HI, NA, and when you're not very interested in something, you'll shrug your shoulders and go, "Meh."

This morning you and I were playing on the floor in your bedroom—I was hiding the phone and you were crawling all over my torso and legs to find it—and you suddenly stopped, your face very close to mine, and you leaned in and pressed your nose to my cheek. We stayed in that position for several spectacular seconds, a hesitation that altered history, a moment so intimate it felt like it could end wars. I could feel you grinning on my skin, and even though I wanted to scoop you up and cover you in kisses I let you hold your face there for as long as you would. I know there are only a handful of moments like that in life. Thank you for that one.

Love,
Mama

Dear Leta,

Tomorrow you turn fifteen months old. You've got two or three or fifteen teeth coming in all at the same time, and the only things that seem to soothe your pain are cold pickles.

Your favorite thing to do now is play with boxes, opening and closing every flap, and doors, pushing them closed and then opening them. Sometimes we'll open the front door so that the dog can look out the screen door and you'll close the door on him, his body cut in half. Remarkably he doesn't mind this at all, barely even notices it really because at least you're not sticking your fingers up his nose or sitting RIGHT NEXT TO HIM as he eats his dinner, both of you on all fours staring mesmerized into the bowl. Last night your father and I caught Chuck sneaking into your room to sleep. We were simultaneously horrified and touched, scared he would wake you but thankful that he loves you enough that he wants to be near you.

About a week ago you started putting weight onto your legs. I honestly never thought I would see you in such a position, standing there holding on to something without someone propping you up. For many months I have been living with the feeling that someone has been gripping my lungs, and last week I took a huge, relaxing breath. I am so proud of you. I am so excited to see you pull yourself up and explore things from a newer, higher perspective. I think this is one of the many times when I will be learning from you, this lesson being that I need to stop worrying about what comes next and simply enjoy what you're giving me now. So what if you can't walk yet, you can put a diaper on your head and laugh about it. I can show you a pen you have never seen and you think I'm some sort of magician: SUCH AN AMAZING CREATION, A PEN. Before I know it you're going to be at an age where you'll be embarrassed to even be associated with me, but right now you can wipe your nose on my shirt and rub your head in it. This is what you're giving me now, the chance to be a mother to a baby, snot and all.

Love,
Mama

Dear Leta,

You father and I left you with Grandmommy for five days while we attended Uncle Shan and Aunt Sydney's wedding. The first two days away were thrilling, because we got to sleep in past 6:00 a.m. And then I started to miss you inexplicably and achingly. At first I was mad about this because we had paid an exorbitant amount of money to Delta Airlines to take us away from you, to get some quality US time, and there I was spending our US time pining for YOU. But then I started seeing other kids your age and thinking about how big or little you were in comparison and I realized that my life has been changed forever, in the sense that I missed you more than I ever missed my old life. I thought about your incessant babbling, your obsessive-compulsive way of opening and closing boxes, the way you REFUSE to keep any hair-restraining device in place on your head. On the plane ride home we saw a girl two days older than you who had not one hair on her head, and I turned to your father and said, "Our daughter, I think she has all the hair in the world for all the babies."

Grandmommy brought you to the airport to pick us up, and when we turned the corner to see you sitting there in her arms you looked at us like, "Wait a minute. Don't I . . . know you?" You then reached out for me and hugged me. I held you and smelled the infant sweat on your neck, so glad to be back in your arms, to have your crazy hair tickling my face. On the way to pick up Chuck I sat in the front seat turned around, just staring at you, memorizing all your features again like flash cards. We tried to get you to say Mama and Daddy, but instead you sat there bleating a string of the most complicated consonants and vowels that could not be re-created by any modern recording device, an alien language that made perfect sense to you as indicated by your hand gestures and dramatic pauses. Then we played our screaming game where you scream and then I scream just like you and then you scream just like me, and this goes on and on while your father navigates traffic. The game always ends when your father looks at me and asks, "So . . . you like this game? Because I'm not so sure this game is all that fun."

You'll now drink from a straw but not from a sippy cup. One day you'll eat two hot dogs for lunch, the next day nothing. One day you'll like going to the park, the next day you act as if driving to the park is like driving over a cliff to your death. You want to be picked up, you want to be put down. You want that book, no, THAT book, NO THAT BOOK! GOD! THHHHAAAAAAT BOOK. I imagine that this is what it's like to be married to a mean drunk.

But you know what? I'm having a lot of fun. We'll play together in your room for hours in the morning taking your shoes out of their boxes and stacking them in little shoe walls. You'll use my body as your personal jungle gym, always crawling back over me if you go anywhere in the room. And when we do find a book that you can agree on and you hand it to me and sit in my lap and listen as I read each and every page, often looking up at my face to see how the words come out of my mouth, I remember people telling me that it would get so much better and I have a feeling that this is what they were talking about.

Love,
Mama

Dear Leta,

Over the weekend you turned seventeen months old. We celebrated by taking you to a huge swimming pool for your first real swimming experience, and while you took to the water without any fuss, you were much more interested in the sunscreen bottle we bought on the way to the pool. You spent almost four hours of your life that day putting the cap on and then pulling it off again, again, and then again. We couldn't feed you or take off your clothes without separating you from the sunscreen cap and bottle, and there was a moment when I thought, *Why can't* we just let her sleep in her wet swim diaper?

Yesterday was the Fourth of July, one of the few days a year the government says we can all sleep in, so why did you wake up at 5:30 a.m.? Usually when you wake up that early we let you talk yourself back to sleep until at least 6:00, but this time, this day of government-sanctioned sleeping in, you screamed from your room, "MAAAMA!" And when that didn't work you tried, "NOOOOOOOOOO!" And then when that didn't work you commenced shaking your crib like the bars of a cage. When I ran into your room you were standing at the end of the bed, your dimpled fists propelling the crib forward, and you instantly yelled, "Hiiiiiiiiiiiiiiii!"

Words you know how to say: hi, mama, bo, no, dank ooh, hi, owwee, hi, dada, hi, NOOOO, hi. Number of times you utter each: at least ninety per minute.

One morning last week you suddenly and without warning realized how to open cabinet doors, and upon returning from the bathroom I found you scurrying like a hoarding squirrel across the floor toward your bedroom with a bottle of Windex tucked under your arm. When I took that bottle away from you, the sound of your disappointment registered on seismographs at Caltech in Pasadena.

What I'm trying to say is, when people ask me about my week or my day, instead of complaining like the old me would do, I say, "She calls me Mama now. I never knew that word could be so amazing."

Love,
Mama

Dear Leta,

Today you turn eighteen months old. Did you know that all I ever wanted was a baby who would snuggle with me and grow up to be a starting forward on a professional basketball team? This month, YOU'VE STARTED SNUGGLING! One goal down, one to go.

I fed you a container of strawberry yogurt and anybody would have thought that I was feeding you liquid happiness, so I went to Costco and bought 4,000 containers of strawberry yogurt. All 4,000 containers are still sitting in the refrigerator because I didn't get the memo that food only tastes good once. You won't even eat French fries. FRENCH FRIES, Leta. I promise you that there will come a day when you will look back on your eighteenth month and you will lament ALL THOSE FRENCH FRIES you could have eaten without guilt.

Sesame Street is now our favorite television show. Both you and I could sit and watch it for hours. Your babysitter and I know entire skits by heart and can act them out for you, even though you look at us strangely like, Stop, you're not doing it right, please just turn the real thing back on. The best part is when you watch it while lounging on the couch like it's the end of a really rough day at work. Oh, and when you hum along with the songs and move your shoulders up and down, I just *know* that this is the beginning of your break-dancing career.

Your vocabulary has exploded in the last few weeks, but there is nothing you like saying better than Mama. This is simultaneously heartwarming and heart-wrenching because, hey! You know who I am. Except, rarely do you ever say Mama as if you are going to follow that word with something nice like, My! How you smell like a flower! Instead you say it like a beer-bellied construction worker who wants his dinner *now*, and so he screams, "WOMAN! Bring me them there pork rinds!" The part where he says WOMAN!, that's how you say Mama.

You've made a lot of progress in terms of walking upright with assistance, moving from coffee table to couch and back without freaking out. You can walk relatively long distances while we hold both your hands, but you still prefer crawling and demanding to be carried. Yesterday you heard three of the little girls who live on our street playing in the neighbor's yard and you crawled to the door to let us know that you wanted to be wherever that action was. I've never seen you giggle so heartily as when you watched those girls run around chasing each other, and for several minutes you had your father run with you after them, holding your hands so you wouldn't topple over. It was a pretty funny scene, your father running around holding the hands of his Mini-Me.

I had to hold back my tears because I wanted you to be able to run with them by yourself. I know you will be able to soon, but this also makes me sad. I'm torn. I see that you want to play, and yet, I never thought this was going to happen, that you'd be old enough to hear their laughter and want to be a part of it. I always thought you'd be this caterpillar that I'd have to carry around in a car seat. And yet, you're here, right on the cusp of this scary socialized network called friends, a world full of happiness and a lot of heartache, and I don't feel ready to send you into it. Once you start walking you won't ever stop, and you won't ever understand the magnitude of that notion until you have a child of your own.

Growing up, I was very sensitive about this small mole on my forehead, but it wasn't lost on me that this mole made me unique and was very much a part of my appearance. When I was a kid I used to imagine that one day when I had children, I would teach them that if they ever felt lonely and needed a hug or kiss, they could come up to me and touch the mole on my forehead and I would give them as many kisses as they needed and then more. It would make having this mole worth the teasing I endured in my youth.

Last week I was teaching you about your nose and your mouth and your eyes, and you were able to mimic me when I touched each feature. Just as I was about to go back to the nose you stopped and got this puzzled look on your face and then you reached up and touched my mole like, Do I have one of those, too? Without hesitation I smothered you in kisses and you laughed with your entire body. Now, whenever we do the face game you go straight for the mole on my forehead and I kiss you and then you stretch your arms out and hug me. Leta, you will never know how many years of my life you have healed with this one gesture. Thank you.

Love,
Mama
(WOMAN!)

Dear Leta,

During the past month we have had a hard time keeping up with your vocabulary. You seem to pick up a new word or a new sound every day. Just the other night Papaw was talking to you in a Donald Duck voice and you tried your hardest to imitate the sound except it came out sounding more like a lion than a duck. You get an A for effort, though. I have been trying to teach you to tell me UP and DOWN to let me know when you want me to pick you up and put you down, but it wasn't until I had to put you into a time-out a couple of weeks ago that the cogs all clicked. Right after I told you not to throw the purple My Little Pony you chucked it probably ten feet across the room. I picked you up, told you that I had warned you not to throw things, and put you in your high chair facing the wall for one minute and thirty seconds. That was probably the longest minute and a half of my life, and when it was over I walked over to you, explained why I had put you there, and asked if you wanted up. And I swear the Earth split open underneath our house and swallowed the neighborhood as you pulled a roar out of the ground and yelled, "UUUUUUUUUUUUUU UUUUUPPPPPPPPPP!" I tried not to laugh, but YOU SPOKE!

You're also very good at saying HI and BYE, especially the latter when your father is about to leave for work. You and I are usually sitting in the living room together watching the morning news when your father leaves for work, and when you see him drape his bag over his arm you start screaming, "BYE-BYE! BYE-BYE! BYE-BYE!" Whenever I answer the phone you start saying BYE-BYE before I even say hello because you know it's coming at some point. And whenever I come up from the basement when the babysitter is here you crawl over to me and when I pick you up you turn to her and say, "BYE-BYE! BYE-BYE! BYE-BYE!" like, "My mother is back, you can leave now. GO." Secretly, very deep down inside, I totally want to high-five you.

One night this month we were standing in line at the grocery store buying a few things for a neighborhood barbecue when your father ran to grab a couple of bags of ice. Before he could get back, though, two other people showed up in line behind us and we were all waiting for your very slow father to return, so I yelled across the store, "JAAAAAAAAHHHHHHN!" in three distinct syllables. Right after I finished yelling his name you smiled and yelled, "JAAAH!" And I thought that was the most awesome trick ever, getting you to call your father by his first name. Your father didn't find it so awesome, but that made it even more awesome for me, and for the next several hours I prompted you to say his name over and over again. Then a few days later we were all sitting in the car together when I turned to you and asked you to say his name. Except this time you looked up at me and said, "DAD." The consonants in that word had never been so firm, and your father had this awful look on his face: one of victory and triumph.

When Papaw moved here to Utah a few weeks ago he dropped off some boxes of toys that I used to play with when I was very little, including an entire box of Strawberry Shortcake dolls dressed in all their original outfits and shoes. I didn't know that my father had kept them, but I'm so glad he did because I used to daydream about having a daughter of my own who would one day play with my toys. At first you didn't know what to make of the dolls, you couldn't turn their pages and read them. But slowly over the last few weeks they've become your favorite toys, and not only will you crawl around with them in both your hands, but the babysitter has taught you how to hug them and call them your "babies." It's an amazing thing to witness, you holding my toys in your tiny hands, and it's nothing like I ever imagined it would be. None of this is. You don't look like I imagined you would look, nor do you sound like I daydreamed you would sound. Motherhood is not at all like the image I had in my head for decades. It's so different, so phenomenally different, and what a marvelous surprise.

Love,
Mama

MONTH TWENTY

Dear Leta,

You're friendly with new people, at least after you've climbed my body like a monkey while playing bashful. You oddly like to share your toys (on your terms) and will spend hours figuring out how something is put together: how do things open, how do they close, can it be punctured, how loud does this go? Last week I made you this toy out of a bowl and a set of marbles and you'd spend hours dumping the marbles out of the bowl and watching them scatter in different directions across the floor. You found the sound and the mess EXHILARATING.

I can't stop gushing. I don't wait for people to ask me about you, I go on and talk about how delightful you make my day just by reaching up to me in the morning. And then I go ahead and tell them about how we assume that having someone pee on us would be totally mortifying, but when it's our own kid, and she's half-naked and her hair is matted to her head in perpendicular angles, we're just so thankful for the memory.

Love,
Mama

Dear Leta,

Today you turn twenty-one months old. Last week your father and I made a huge mistake by encouraging you to play Sesame Street games on the computer. I say mistake because you became instantly addicted and when we took it away you got the twitches. It doesn't help that we have more computers in our house than in the entire state of Arkansas, and every time you turn around you are bombarded with the temptation. You ask for it with "Melmo?" And when we say that Melmo is sleeping you say, "Melmo?" And when we say Not now you say, "Melmo?" And at that point your bottom lip starts quivering and I just give in. The good news is that you want Computer Melmo bad enough that you've started saying please. The even better news is that even though the sign for please is a circular hand motion at the top of the chest, you say please by scratching your underarms like an ape and saying, "Oh koh." Where you learned that I have no idea but keep it up and I'll give you anything.

We've learned that when you hear the first note of a specific episode of *Sesame Street*, the one where everyone gathers to sing about something being in the air today, something that makes them want to sing, you race to the middle of the living room floor and start belting out words as loud and as off-key as you can sing them, SIIINGS and DAAAYS and SAAAAYS. I now can't sleep at night because all I hear is that song on repeat with your vocal accompaniment, but I'm not complaining. I'm reminded that you have made me live my life differently, more slowly. I can't pass the toy section in the grocery store without stopping, without taking the time to see if they have anything new. I can't pass a tree whose leaves have turned red without plucking one off and sticking it in my pocket. You have slowed me down and brought me closer to the kid I used to be. You have made me learn every word to that *Sesame Street* song, and not only do I forgive you for that, I will sit on the floor and sing it with you.

Love,
Mama

Dear Leta,

This month you have stopped calling Elmo Melmo and have instead embraced your Southern heritage and started referring to him as Yelma. It always sounds like a question: Yelma? Thar's a hole in mah bucket, Yelma? Most words now start with a Y—up is yup, open is yopen, again is yageen, and nap is nyap. You'll repeat anything we say. One morning you and I were playing with a small bouncy ball when I accidentally sent it flying underneath the piano. Before I could stop myself I muttered, "SHIT SHIT SHIT," after which you immediately said in the same tone, "THIT THIT THIT." Just then across the room, the dog sat down as if given a command.

About a month and a half ago you took your first steps. Since then you haven't done much walking, if any at all. I thought that once you discovered the free-dom of walking you would take off *flying*. But you are instinctively tentative, and because you are old enough now to understand that you fall much farther when you walk, you are far more reluctant to try it than someone much younger who doesn't yet understand cause and effect. In the last few days, however, you've shown so much more interest in doing it yourself, and your father and I have screamed ourselves hoarse trying to encourage you. The other night you were walking back and forth between us when the dog came upstairs to see what all the unnecessary screaming was about, couldn't we be quiet? When he saw you coming at him upright with your E.T. waddle he whipped his head around to give me a look that said, "When did this happen? And when were you going to tell me?"

Two nights ago you came down with your first fever. You aren't normally a cuddly kid. In fact, trying to hug you is like trying to spoon a cactus, but the moment that fever hit you, you clung to my neck with the weight of an anchor. For several hours we sat together, your body draped across my chest, the heat of your fever pasting your hair to my neck. I used to hold you that way for days at a time when you were only weeks old. It was the only way you would sleep, and you made these noises that kept me awake all night, grunts and snorts and coughs that sounded like you'd been smoking for fifty years. The other night, though, you were entirely silent, as still as the moment they first laid you on my chest in the delivery room.

Sometimes I think that my memory is going to dull and that in ten or fifteen years I won't remember specifically what it felt like to see you for the first time, that the perfect moment of meeting each other and not knowing each other's weaknesses will be lost as we find out that the other one isn't perfect.

But as you clung to my neck the other night I felt it again, an innocence laid bare in both of us, and I realized that without even knowing it, we continue to pull each other back to those first few minutes together, just a mother and her child. I understand now that it's not a matter of forgetting what it felt like, it's a matter of being reminded by living it over and over again.

Love,
Mama

Dear Leta,

Today you turn twenty-three months old. Over the weekend we watched a few hours of home videos we've taken during the last couple of years, and I think you've finally found something you love more than Elmo: yourself. Anytime you watched yourself perform something extraordinary, like a front flip in bed or putting the lens cap on the camera while I was filming, you giggled maniacally and demanded to see it, "Ah-gin! Ah-gin!" We watched you turn front flips over and over ah-gin until your father finally said, "No, we're going to watch something else now, Leta."

Your love for yourself, though, hasn't diminished your love for Elmo one bit. During one sequence of video you saw yourself walking around hugging Elmo to your chest and I think you thought he might be trapped in the television. You threw your body against the screen and pounded it with both your open palms. We had to fast-forward through that whole sequence so you didn't have a heart attack. You will often refer to your other toys as Elmo-this or that. Your stuffed bunny is Elmo-Bunny; your stuffed giraffe is Elmo-Raffe. You have on more than one occasion referred to me as Elmo-Mama, and while I have tolerated most of the things you have thrown my way, I'm not about to let Elmo have any of the credit for bringing you into the world.

Turns out that you already know the entire alphabet, and the only explanation for this is that you pay close attention to *Sesame Street*, that you are thriving and learning things *despite* your lazy parents. One afternoon I was in the middle of the living room floor coloring with you when I started to write your name. You looked at the letters I had written and said out loud while pointing to each one, "L-E-T-A." Thinking that I was hearing voices in my head I wrote out my own name to see if you would recognize any other letters. Before I could even ask you what each one was you spelled out my name—from the H-E-A to the T-H-E-R—and then I frantically looked around the room to see who was playing this joke on me.

I wrote letter after letter and you identified each one. "Which one is this?"

"K."

"And this one?"

"Q."

I even tried to trick you by throwing in some numbers. "What's this letter?"

"10."

"Someone's feeding you the answers. I know you won't know this one."

"13."

Except it sounded like "Ter-ten," and at that point I wondered what else you knew and how long we could hide you from the government. After showing you off to your father, we agreed that we would take full credit when anyone asks us how you know your numbers and letters so early.

You often sing your ABC's and stop after T because the rest of the song doesn't interest you. I don't blame you, after T it's all downhill.

A few days ago after getting you dressed for the day I asked you to walk with your father to the living room so that I could go Pee-Pee. At first you didn't want to, but your father finally convinced you to let me be alone, that sometimes human beings like to be by themselves when they go Pee-Pee. As you walked away, I heard you sing, "L-M-N-O-Pee-Pee."

A few weeks ago you started calling me Mom. Not Mama or Mommy, but Mom. I thought I had at least six or seven years. When you say it you sound like you're fifteen years old and *so* embarrassed. I'm only a

little bothered by this, because at least you're not calling me Heather.

I don't mind being called Mom as much as I mind how fast you are becoming a little girl. I didn't think I was supposed to notice because I see you every day, but sometimes I wake up and you look a little taller or your cheeks are a little leaner. All your hair fits into one rubber band at the top of your head now, and throughout the day as strands fall around your face you look like a Renaissance painting, you're so beautiful. Sometimes I see you playing across the room by yourself and I will selfishly interrupt you and ask you if you'd like me to scratch your back. You'll look up and say, "Scatch!" and walk over and lie belly-down across my lap so that I can scratch your back and the palms of your hands. My mom used to scratch my back just like this, and I used to worry that she would grow tired of it because I wanted her to do it so much. But now I think she was worried that maybe I would get tired of it, because she liked to scratch my back. So I want you to know just in case you ever get worried, I won't ever get tired of this. You can lie in my lap whenever you need to, hopefully more often.

Love,
Mama

Dear Leta,

Happy Birthday number two! In the last month you have perfected the skill of walking and it has changed our lives completely, and not just because you can flee the scene of a crime now. Walking has triggered my mother's over-achieving DNA in your genes and you no longer consider the television worthy of your precious, limited time. Who needs Elmo when you've got legs? What we would give to have you sit still for more than a minute at a time now, and don't think we haven't tried to encourage in you an unhealthy obsession with various cartoons, any cartoon, please just stop running to the bathroom and yanking toilet paper off the roll. We leave the television on at all times hoping that something will grab your attention, and when you show the smallest bit of interest in something it's a mad dash to the TiVo remote to press Record and save as many copies as possible.

Recently you've been experiencing another phase of separation anxiety, and I am rarely able to leave the room without a Shakespearean tragedy unfolding at my feet. While this can be somewhat crippling—I can't put on a pair of pants without first detaching your body from my leg—it is also something I'm trying to enjoy for what it is. You imitate every move I make, every cough and sneeze. You study my daily routine and I have seen you pretend to squirt hair product into your hands, rub them together, and then smooth it across the top of your head. You're always asking to wear my bracelets, and when I drape them over your wrist you jingle them softly and then prance around the house as if you have just been crowned Ruler of the World.

If you are acting grumpy and we ask you what is wrong you answer, "Wrong." If I point to your father and ask, "Who is that?" you answer, "That." If we want you to say please before we give you something I'll ask you, "What do you say?" and you'll answer, "Say." This is more funny that it is frustrating, I have to admit, and it has brought some of our own habits into stark relief. A few weeks ago I was getting dressed for the day and I walked into the bedroom wearing nothing but my underwear. You and your father were sitting on the bed reading books, and when you saw me walk through the door you assessed what I was wearing and then let out a guttural imitation of a construction worker: " H e e e e e E E E E E E E E E Y Y Y Y Y !

YeaaaaaaHHHHHHH!" Your father laughed and then admitted, "I couldn't have said it better myself."

Earlier this week I had to catch a plane to California, and even though I checked in over forty-five minutes before departure they told me they didn't have a seat for me. They had overbooked the plane and to compensate they volunteered me to stick around the airport for another six hours to catch a later flight. I was livid, particularly because the whole trip was going to span less than twenty-four hours and I would have to spend the first six of those waiting for another plane. I immediately walked over to the customer service desk and asked for a refund on the ticket, and because I had already had a monumentally bad day I bit my upper lip to muffle an almost unnoticeable string of tears. I was upset that the situation seemed so unfair, upset that I was standing there alone under the weight of that injustice and no one else had an obligation to care.

I think the man who took my complaint saw that my lower lip was trembling, because he told me to wait one second as he disappeared down the corridor. A few moments later he returned to tell me that they had found a seat for me and that I needed to hurry, they were holding the plane. I took off flying, my suitcase turning flips behind me, and as I ran down the indoor tarmac someone suddenly called out my name. I stopped suddenly to scan the faces in the crowd only to see my mother standing twenty feet in front of me, my beautiful, perfect mother. It seems ridiculous now, but in that moment it seemed as if she had appeared out of thin air, that she had dropped out of heaven. When I saw the features in her face, the way her cheekbones meet her thin nose in symmetrical angles, her milky complexion peeking out of the black of her business suit, I realized that everything was going to be okay. That was one of the most spiritual moments of my life.

I wanted to tell you that story because that is my hope for you, that no matter how far away you go or how different we may become—I know it's going to happen, it's only a matter of time—when you see my face you will find strength. Look for me.

Love,
Elmo-Mama

Dear Leta,

This month you have finally become enamored of walking upright and have walked circles around the house so often that there are visible tread marks in the hardwood floor. You love to yank me by the hand and say, "Walk!" to get me to walk laps with you, and one night last week we went outside and walked up and down the block for over an hour. Usually, though, when you take me by the hand for these walks we always end up in the kitchen right in front of the medicine cabinet where we keep your Gummi vitamins, and you'll pull on my arm signaling that We Have Arrived At Our Destination. "Min!" you'll say, and even if I indicate that you've already had your vitamin today you continue to repeat that word—min, min, min—until I relent and let you pick out another one from the bottle.

Recently your imagination has exploded and you love to play pretend. You often carry around Potty Elmo—one of four Elmo dolls you have, he wears a diaper and when he says that he needs to go to the bathroom you have to sit him on his potty posthaste or he sings, "OOPS! Elmo didn't make it to the potty!" which is so annoying that when you aren't looking I punch him in the head—and you're constantly checking his diaper to see if he has gone Poo-Poo. One morning last week I was lying on the couch in the living room and you brought me a blanket, covered me up, and said, "Night-night, Mama." Then you disappeared around the corner only to return with Potty Elmo, whom you tucked under the covers next to me. "Hug Elmo," you commanded. So I hugged Elmo, and then you said night-night again. You kept taking Elmo back around the corner and then returning with him, each time demanding that I hug him. It was a game of Night-Night, and I made the monumental mistake of getting up in the middle of this game without running it by you first. When you saw me standing in the kitchen doorway your face contorted in horror, and after throwing your body headfirst across the room you screamed, "NIIIIIIIIIIIGHT-NIIIIIIIIIIIGHT!"

Your father has started working from home, and in the last month that transition has finally given way to a newer way of life. He's taken over almost all the chores and he's even pretty good at them, even though he did put my sports bra in the dryer and during one of my workouts I lost feeling in both legs because my circulation was being cut off at my boobs. The best part, though, is his relationship with you and how you've responded to all this time he's spent with you. You often call for him when you wake up in the morning or call out his name when you fall. You follow him around the house and want him to sit on the floor and read you books. You often cry when he leaves the room.

I can honestly say that what has happened between you and your father—the way you look at him now, the way you crawl up into his lap and touch his face, that one time when he was crying and you ran to him and wrapped your arms around his neck, that you two have been able to have this time together—that alone is worth everything.

Love,
Mama

Dear Leta,

This month has seen the return of television. You used to be a huge fan of *Sesame Street* but once you learned to walk you had no use for that nonsense, and this made me terribly sad for a few reasons. One, we all stopped sitting still, which is fine for you, you're two and you have the energy. Two, I really started to worry that we were missing out on what was going down on the Street while you and I were running around the house checking all your stuffed animals for poopy diapers.

So your father and I worked hard and now you will momentarily sit still in front of *Monsters, Inc.* or *Blue's Clues*. You ask for Mon-eek or Coos-coos, and your father and I then have maybe fifteen minutes tops to use the bathroom or lie on the floor and twitch before you realize that there is perhaps something in the house that hasn't had its diaper checked for poop recently, and it's off to the races again. Your father and I are not easily deterred, though, and last week while cleaning out the car your father brought the car seat into the house for a few hours. This BLEW YOUR MIND, and so we used that novelty to our advantage. For several hours that day you requested that we buckle you into that seat right in the middle of the living room floor. No problem! How about a movie? And since you're buckled in, why not get comfortable? Here's your blanket and some yummy snacks.

A few weeks ago your father and I went to Texas to a conference and we left you with Papaw. We delivered you to him in working order, but when he returned you to us you were broken. For two years we have culti-vated a morning routine with you, one in which we wake up slowly while lounging in bed, watching the morning news, and eating dry cereal. We worked hard for two years to get you used to that pace, but the morning after we got back from Texas you wanted to start the day immediately. It was still dark outside, and even though I hadn't yet had coffee you wanted to start checking Elmo for a poopy diaper NOW. I wondered what my dad had done to you and then realized he probably had you up at the crack of dawn scrubbing the grout in the bathroom tile or vacuuming the floor mats in his car.

We have slowly retrained you to start the day more softly, but it hasn't been easy. This morning, however, your father brought you into bed with us when you woke up, and you snuggled right up into my neck. This was strange because I am used to the duck-pecking of your morning demands. Your father realized the significance of the moment, too, and climbed into bed right next to you, his hand on your back, the three of us an Armstrong sandwich.

We all lay there for an hour dozing and cuddling. As you started to wake up I reached over and started scratching your forearm, and then you stuck your arm straight in the air as an indication that I should scratch the parts of your arm that I would otherwise be unable to access, kind of like what Chuck does when I reach down to rub his belly and he falls over on his side with a thud. I continued scratching your arm for a few minutes until you grabbed my hand and stopped me, forcing my arm back against my chest. "Scratch Mama," you said and then ran your fingers up and down my arm. It paralyzed me, the way you gave back to me, and I had a hard time breathing because that's the type of thing we spend our whole life hoping for.

Love,
Mama

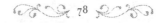

Dear Leta,

I'm not sure what has made this last month so special, but I find myself gushing to everyone I know that this age has so far been the best one. This is something I have seen other parents do, talk about the age they liked best, but until now I haven't been able to jump in with much enthusiasm. Some like it best when the baby is still very small and chubby and edible, others like it when they are old enough to pay their own rent, preferably in another city. And it's not that I haven't had fun until now, because I have, it's just that you are right now a perfect blend of baby and person, not too much of either.

You've also got this amazing sense of humor and somehow have the maturity to know how to use it. Often we will be sitting at the table having a meal, and I will look up at you only to see that you have your eyes crossed again. When I was a kid there was this urban legend that if you crossed your eyes and someone came along and hit you in the back of the head while you were doing it your eyes would stay crossed like that forever. I have never stopped believing in that possibility, so when I ask you kindly to uncross your eyes you giggle and say, "I'm funny, huh?" One of your new habits is to mimic our everyday activities like sweeping the floor and sticking the keys into the lock on the front door. When we come home from running an errand and I unlock the door I have to hand you the keys so you can pretend to do the same. You'll often mumble exasperated nonsense to yourself in the same tone that I do when I open the door. One night last week while you and I were playing with a deck of cards, you suddenly hopped up and ran into the kitchen with the seven of hearts. I followed you in to see what you were up to, and you had gone over to our side-by-side refrigerator to run the playing card through the slot between the doors, like a credit card. Then you handed it back to me and asked for another card. Why? Was that one rejected? Could you please try *one* more time, because I don't have my checkbook on me.

This month we bought you a small art table and chairs perfect for someone your size. It is your favorite place in the house now, and you often grab my finger with your small hand to lead me to it. "Color?" you'll ask, except it sounds like CUH-YAH, and I'll plop down into the too small chair to join you in scribbling with the washable markers. Your father was adamant when we bought art supplies that we would encourage you to use them however you liked as long as you didn't destroy furniture. He wanted you to be able to use as much paper as you liked and also as much ink as your masterpieces required, because he wasn't given that type of support when he was fostering his creative side. So I agreed, and even though the practical side of me sometimes flinches when you go through an entire tablet of paper in one coloring session, I mostly rejoice that you're showing so much interest in creating something. So when you started coloring your arms, I applauded you. You were just expanding your canvas, right? But your father walked in and was all WHY ARE YOU LETTING HER DO THAT? And I was all BUT YOU SAID TO ENCOURAGE THE ARTIST IN HER. And he was all YES, BUT THAT WAS BEFORE I REALIZED HER ART WOULD REQUIRE REALLY TEDIOUS CLEAN-UP, AND NOW I MUST GO GRAPPLE WITH THE HORRIFYING REALIZATION THAT I HAVE BECOME MY FATHER.

Last month my cousin had his first child, a little girl, your second cousin, and a few weeks later when I called to see how he was doing, he talked about what a surreal experience it was to have this new person in their home.

He said that when they were still in the hospital, he felt the usual pride a father does about a newborn daughter, that she was the most beautiful baby in the world. But then, he said, when he came home he realized that things were so crazy in the hospital that his feeling then about her beauty was totally subjective, that he thought she was the most beautiful baby only because she was his daughter. Now that they were home and he felt clear-headed he couldn't believe just how pretty she was, and he felt that he could make an objective, scientific assessment that she was, indeed, the most beautiful baby in the world. And he said all this to me with the seriousness and authority of an expert.

I laughed quite a bit about that conversation, because that's sort of a cliché about parents. We all believe that our children are the most beautiful children in the world. But the thing is, what no one really talks about is the fact that we all really believe it. I, too, believe it, that you are the most beautiful child in the world, and as absurd as my cousin was being about his own baby, I'm not being absurd about you. I feel it so strongly, so completely, that even the most rational part of me can't help but feel that it's true: you are objectively the most wonderful, beautiful person in the world.

Love,
Mama

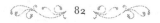

Dear Leta,

Over the weekend you turned twenty-eight months old. I think it's about time we address the issue of your hair, considering that every picture we take of you makes it look like I do nothing but follow you around with balloons and rub them on your head.

We have very few photographs of your hair looking tidy because, as your stepgrandma has said, styling your hair is exactly like trying to wrap a rubber band around a wad of Jell-O. It just falls out everywhere a few seconds after I comb it into place. Add to that the fact that you have more hair on your head right now than most people will ever grow in a lifetime, and you can see how it's easy for me to throw my hands up in defeat.

Your love for walks has grown to an obsession this month, and we spend many hours a day in the front yard or walking up and down our street. We love taking these walks because it forces us to slow down and appreciate very small and simple things as you bend down to examine your world. You're often exploring holes in the sidewalk with your fingers, or stopping to watch a trail of ants. This morning I walked out the front door to lounge on the porch, and you followed me until you got to the lip of the front step and realized you didn't have your shoes on. "SHOOOOES!" you screamed. "WHERE ARE YOU!"

Now you take a three-hour nap in the afternoon and rarely put up a fuss, except yesterday when you reached into your arsenal of excuses and tried everything to get out of it. Your father and I listened on the monitor as you said, "Watch Elmo? . . . No? Okay. Go outside! . . . No? How about crackers? No? Water!" I admire your determination, Leta, but if you want to see results you're going to need to get a little more creative.

One of our favorite parts of the day with you is bath time, if only because you are never more excited. Each time I mention that it's time for your bath you take off running, and when I catch up with you in the bathroom you're trying to throw your leg over the side of the bathtub, even though I haven't started running the water or taken your clothes off. For several months, you hated the part where we washed your hair, and that was totally my fault. I wanted to try out a new adult shampoo on you because I thought it might *revitalize the texture* of your hair and make it smell like freshly picked mountain strawberries. But it burned your eyes, and even when we switched back to the harmless baby shampoo, you were still extremely wary of having water poured over your head, so we've had to come up with ways to get you to cooperate. Lately we've been tacking letters up high on the walls of the bathtub and asking you to identify them, and while your head is tilted back, we quickly rinse the suds out of your hair. The other night we tried this trick again, and it worked so well you wouldn't stop. You recognized the A, and then the G, and then the X, and even after your hair was rinsed, you stood up out of the water and pointed to each letter sticking to the tub.

"You're smart, little one," your father said as he shook his head. "Can you say, 'I'm smart'?"

You giggled and said, "I'm fart."

We've never laughed so hard or been more aware that there is nothing in life more wonderful than this, our family, you who have truly made us one.

Love,
Mama

Dear Leta,

This week you turned twenty-nine months old. I will remember this month as the onset of the expletive. We were sitting on the porch moments after I had watered my potted plants. Without warning, a puddle of water from one of the pots snaked its way under your hand, and you jerked it up and yelled, "What the hay-yull?" I couldn't figure out where you had learned to say that, until it dawned on me: it's because your father doesn't know how to cook a frozen pizza.

One morning last week, we were all lying in bed together with our laptops. Your toy laptop was given to you by my mother for Christmas, and it features several spelling games where you're asked what letter is missing in a word. We thought you'd love to press the many buttons on its keyboard, but we never thought you'd be able to participate in the games for at least a few years. This was one of those many instances when you have proved that maybe our expectations of you are much too modest, because that morning you showed us that you can spell many of the words on that computer. All I ever wanted was a child who would grow up and breathe air, and look!

At one point the computer asked you what letter was missing in the word ROBOT. You accidentally pushed the E instead of the O, and when it said, "Uh-oh, try again!" you bit your lower lip and said, "Shit!" Both your father and I froze, afraid that any reaction would be the wrong one, and he asked me what you had just said, in case he had heard it wrong. Before I could confirm his worst fears, you turned your head to look straight at him and said, "I said SHIT!" As if to say, Because you didn't hear me clearly the first time, Father.

This month the weather has been cooperative enough that we've been able to introduce you to water in its many wonderful forms: pools, fountains, lakes, and sprinklers. The one we had the most success with was the fountain at the local outdoor mall where, after only a few minutes of hesitation, you ran headfirst into one giant stream shooting up out of the ground. I hadn't prepared for the possibility that you would be so enthusiastic, hadn't packed a bathing suit, so I let you run around in nothing but a blue swim diaper. When I noticed that every other kid was wearing a bathing suit, I pulled your father to the side and asked him quietly why ours was the only one halfway naked, were there laws against letting your children run around in public looking as if they were homeless?

Earlier this week we visited a small reservoir near my mother's cabin in the desert, and we hoped you would react as happily as you did last year when we took you to a beach. Instead, you freaked out when a handful of wet sand washed over your foot and clung to the spaces between your toes. You hated it so much that you demanded that your father carry you back to your towel, and then you spent more than ten minutes cleaning off your foot with a wet wipe. This didn't necessarily surprise me, because you cannot stand to have anything remotely messy on your face or your hands, and you spend more time wiping the crumbs off your face during mealtime than you do eating.

A couple of weeks ago you and I were standing outside talking to the neighbors during that enchanted part of the day when the sun is setting and kids are running around trying to pack in as much of life as they can before they are forced to go to bed. Every kid on the block was outside chasing every other, laughing, and swinging from the trees. You stood close to me, your arms wrapped around my leg, and watched the surrounding excitement as if it were a traveling circus. Suddenly a neighbor's sprinklers went off, and that circus converged like a black hole onto that wet yard.

You gasped, let go of my leg, and waddled off with the others to feel the spray on your arms and face. The ten seconds that it took you to walk over and play in the water just about knocked me over with their significance: you were walking *on your own* to be with other children.

I will never take for granted the fact that you are able to do that now, able to move your legs normally, able to take yourself where you want to go. There is no amount of money, no fortune or success in this world that could make me feel as blessed as I did in those ten seconds.

Love,
Mama

Dear Leta,

Yesterday you turned thirty months old. For the past few weeks you have enjoyed nothing more than chewing a piece of gum. I'm sure other mothers would be horrified to know that I let you chew gum at your age, but both your father and I chewed gum even earlier than this. You could say it's a talent we've passed on. Here's where I apologize that the talent wasn't something more spectular like, say, an operatic singing voice or the ability to solve cold fusion.

Sometimes it is the first thing you ask for when you get up in the morning, a piece of gum, and I have been trying to use your fascination with gum to teach you how to ask for things nicely. Usually you will ask for something, in this instance a piece of gum, a piece of gum, a piece of gum, A PIECE OF GUM! A PIEEEEEEECE OF GUUUUUUUUUUMMMMMM!

Once I've successfully guided you into asking for it the right way—with a please in the original request and maybe a kind word or two about my hair — I'll give you a piece of gum and then check up on you at regular intervals to make sure you haven't swallowed it. I never realized that learning *not* to swallow something would be a skill at which you'd have to work. I can count several times when I have asked you where your gum is, and you've stuck both hands in your mouth to search for it only to give up after thirty seconds and say, "Um, I swallowed it?"

A few weeks ago, you and I attended a music group with twelve other mothers and kids. At one point, the teacher walked around to each child to let them blow bubbles through a straw into a glass of water to demonstrate the musical sound it makes. When she got to you, I watched in slow motion as you reached into your mouth, pulled out your gum, and cupped it like a precious jewel in your left hand.

This month your obsession with keeping your hands clean has reached a new level, and more than once you have touched a piece of food and then refused to eat it because it dared to have a texture. Yesterday you were staring blankly at a plate full of French fries and the moment you dipped one of those fries in ketchup, your entire body went completely rigid. Your father and I had no idea what was going on, maybe you accidentally got a drop of ketchup on your hand, so I immediately handed you a wipe. And I am not making this up, you took that wipe and used it to clean the ketchup off the French fry.

Last week I had to go out of town for several days, and although I have gone on business trips in the past, this one was by far the most difficult in terms of being away from you. Ten minutes after you and your father dropped me off at the airport, I wanted to go back home, and I continued to call your father every hour for the next five days. Each time he would tell me what you two had been doing—swimming in the pool, eating Popsicles on the porch, changing Elmo's diaper—and I felt as if I were missing out on years of your life. During one phone call, you realized that your father was talking to me, and I heard you reach for the phone and say, "I want to get you, Mama." That's how you tell me that you want me to pick you up, want me to hold you when you're hurt or sad. You say it while reaching up to me with both arms open. I sat alone in my hotel room and cried thinking about the few times in my life I will get to hear that from you.

I want to get you, too.

Love,
Mama

Dear Leta,

Many nights your father and I will fall lifeless into bed, and in the moments before we both fall asleep one of us will turn to the other and say, "I want pink gum." Those are the first words out of your mouth every morning, and it's our way of reminding each other of what we have to look forward to, of the reason our lives are really quite wonderful. It's impossible to dwell on the more difficult parts of life when you live with someone who screams in public, "Daddy tooted!"

Mornings are your most talkative time, and after demanding a piece of gum and before I've even lifted you out of the crib, you start asking for various items from the kitchen as if ordering from a menu:

"A cup of water. Big. With ice in it."

"Strawberry coptart. Not hot."

"Chitchen. Four. With mustard. And tetchup."

You will only eat a specific brand of chicken nuggets, ones shaped like the silhouettes of dinosaurs, and in the most recent bag we bought there was one piece that must have gotten caught in the machine at the manufacturing plant. Two dinosaurs had fused into one giant lump, and I actively avoided serving it to you until it was one of the only pieces left. I was hoping that maybe you wouldn't notice the odd piece, and you didn't until you had already dipped it in ketchup and brought it to your mouth. That's when the monstrosity confronted you with its Wrongness, and afterward as I mopped up the mess, your father mentioned that he had avoided serving you that exact piece, too. Do you know how embarrassing it is for someone to realize that they have rearranged their life around a chicken nugget?

Just one day previous to that incident, we were all sitting around the table having lunch together, you and I and your father and the babysitter, when you refused to eat the chicken we had cooked for you. Whether or not you eat a particular meal is going to have very little effect on whether or not you make it to your next birthday, so I no longer spend any energy worrying about this. Your father, however, cannot stifle the DNA given to him by his own father, and when you rebel this way, he feels an irresistible need to prove just how much control he has as a parent, and more importantly, as a man. "Leta!" he said as he gripped the top of the table. "You see all three of us sitting here? We are all your bosses. Mama is your boss, Katey is your boss, Daddy is your boss. Your bosses are telling you to EAT YOUR CHICKEN." It wasn't the most convincing argument he has ever made, but it was probably his loudest. You sat very quietly with your hands in your lap, and after shooting both me and the babysitter a quick look, you pointed straight at your father and said with *tone*, "Mama is the boss OF YOU!"

This month we have spent many afternoons playing with your plastic baby dolls, pushing them around the house in strollers and wrapping them in blankets to keep them warm during the long, cold summer. You love to put together puzzles, draw flowers, jump on the bed, and recite entire books from memory. One day when we had exhausted all your usual activities, I was searching for something to allay your boredom when absentmindedly I stuck a small bouncy ball in my mouth and spit it out like a clown. You thought it was the funniest thing you had ever seen, and so we spent the next hour spitting out bouncy balls. I didn't think anything of it until the next morning when I was working in the basement and I heard the babysitter scream. I ran upstairs to find her hyperventilating, and when I asked what was wrong she said, "Leta put a bouncy ball in her mouth!" You mean, one of those objects that is as perfectly round as the opening in her throat . . . which could lodge itself squarely in her esophagus?

One night last week, we had dinner with my father and arrived home later than your usual bedtime. When we walked in the door, I told you to follow me into the bathroom to get ready for bed, but you protested the way someone your age usually does, with a really dramatic, "Nuh-uh!" and by stomping your itty-bitty feet. I headed to your room to get out your pajamas when I heard your father walk to the front of the house and tell you it was time for bed. "No," you said again, but this time more softly, more reasonably, and then continued, "I'm sitting here for two minutes." Your father yelled from the living room that you had put yourself into a time-out, had moved your chair against the wall and climbed onto it. How could we possibly expect you to go to bed when you are not allowed to get out of that chair? That was an impressive tactic.

I had no idea that you would continue to become more charming, more adorable, more full of surprises. At this age you are like Christmas every morning, always saying something wildly outrageous, often breaking into song in the oddest places. Whenever I talk about you to other people, whenever they ask me how I'm doing with this, I'm not sure I can adequately communicate just how lucky I am to know you.

Love,
Mama

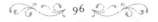

Dear Leta,

This month you took your first plane ride, or at least the first one that counts. The *other* first plane ride of your life happened two years ago, but there's no possible way you will ever remember it. Watching you peek over the ledge of the window and talk about being "up in the sky" was like getting to experience a flight for the first time all over again.

This was also the month of running commentary. A typical morning goes like this:

Me: You awake, little one?

You: CLOTHES ON! CHANGE THE DIAPER! TAKE OFF PAJAMAS! PUT ON PANTS! AND SHIRT! AND SHOES ONS! WITH SOCKS! SOCKS ONS! OKAY?

Me: Yes, we'll put your shoes ons—

You: SHOES ONS! THEN BRUSH TEETH! WITH PASTE! AND WATER! ELMO TOOTH-BRUSH! SAY AHHH! AND BRUSH HAIR! PRETTY HAIR! OKAY?

Me: Okay—

You: THEN WATCH SESS STREET! ON THE COUCH! WITH WATER! AND ICE! IN A CUP! A BIG CUP! AND SIT NEXT TO YOU! OKAY?

Me: Yes, I'll sit next to you, but—

You: AND HAVE BEANS! BROWN BEANS! IN A BOWL! GREEN BOWL! WITH A SPOON! BLUE SPOON! LETA SPOON! MAMA HAVE COFFEE! IN A CUP! BIG CUP! DADDY HAVE ORANGE CUP! PLAY WITH PUZZLES AND READ BOOKS AND GET IN THE CAR AND GO TO THE BOOKSTORE! OKAY?

Me: Okay, but how about I turn on the light first?

What I find interesting is that the older you get, the more your energy level begins to mirror our own. Your father and I are never more content than when we are relaxing on the couch reading books and magazines and websites, our heads curled up into pillows and on each other's shoulders. While we were away on vacation last week, out on the beach or walking through shops or through the park, you frequently asked "to go home and sit on the couch and read books and sit next to you." I knew exactly how you felt, like, this is great and all, nice bridge, cool building, but where's the *couch*?

Love,
Mama

Dear Leta,

We've discovered that you want everything to seem as if you were the one who thought of it first, and many times when we suggest an item of food or a particular activity you will refuse it, only to suggest the same thing about fifteen seconds later. When asked if you'd like chicken for dinner your usual response is a NO! so powerful that it could knock a bird out of a tree. But moments later, you'll suggest that we fix you chicken for dinner with an almost sinister enthusiasm, like, This idea of mine? The chicken for dinner? I bet you didn't think you'd ever give birth to such a fascinating thinker, did you? CHICKEN! FOR *DINNER*! I mean, how *innovative* is that?

One thing we've noticed is how polite and courteous you've become, and you're always saying thank you and please and excuse me at the appropriate times without being prompted to do so. I have had to hammer on some of these concepts over and over, often making you repeat a thank-you because it doesn't count if it's mumbled, but generally you're a really cordial kid who will be the first one in the room to say bless you when someone sneezes. More than once you've even tried to make me feel better about my frequent numbskullery, tried to comfort me in a tender way when I've spilled a glass of orange juice or run into the door jamb with my forehead. "It's okay, Mama," you say as you run to pat reassuringly on my hand. "Not a problem. It could happen to anyone."

In addition to your sympathetic nature you're also very gentle and play very differently from most of your peers. You could sit for hours on the floor in your room putting together puzzles and reading books, whereas most of your friends are much more physical and prefer to hop around and run from room to room. Yesterday you even got mad at someone because she wouldn't sit still on the floor with you, because she wanted to explore the various nooks of our bathroom, and at one point your frustration was so overwhelming that I totally thought you were going to roll your eyes and tell her that she was being so immature.

There was also that time you were playing with a young baby boy in the neighborhood who is considerably younger than you and not yet into doing puzzles. You were fascinated with all the toys in his playroom, but he was much more captivated by you and your hair. While you arranged small figurines around a giant red fire truck, he crawled over to you and climbed up on your back until his left hand was clutching a giant chunk of your hair, his right hand was hanging on your ear, and his mouth was chewing on the back of your shirt. And you sat there and let him do it, presumably because there had to be a good reason for this type of behavior, right? You had no idea babies were so uncivilized, but whatever. Instead of swatting him off or screaming you sat there and let him maul you, and I think you did this because you thought it was the right thing to do, because he was smaller than you and you knew that he didn't know any better. That's a pretty advanced concept for someone your age, and I think you should hold on to that instinct to try and live peacefully with others.

Last week you spent a day and a night with my mother because she wanted to give your father and me some time to get some work done and then go out and have an adult dinner together. The following morning when she brought you home you were so hysterical that on my way to the front door I could hear you crying from the backseat of her car. You did not want your time with her to end, and she sat for over a half hour on our couch with you clinging to her neck, begging her to take you back to her house. This has happened to every grandchild in this family, and my sister's kids used to cry for Grandmommy in the middle of the night. My mother finds all this wildly hilarious, and so I told her that the first time you scream for her in the middle of the night, I'm going to call her right then and tell her to come pick you up. Will it still be funny at 4:00 a.m.? I can't wait to find out.

But I have to admit that I couldn't be happier that you have this relationship with her. I had always hoped it would be this way, and witnessing your dizzying excitement to see her or to see my father is exactly why we moved back to Utah. I don't have memories of my grandparents like the ones you will have of yours. You have spent more time with your grandparents already than I ever got to spend with mine, and the way that they adore you and delight in you is just one of the many reasons you have the best grandparents that life could offer. Watching you turn to my dad, reach up for his hand, and say, "Papaw, come with me," and then seeing how much that touches him, I can say that in moments like those I think he forgives the world everything.

Love,
Mama

Dear Leta,

Yesterday you turned thirty-four months old. In the last few weeks you have forged a remarkable relationship with your five-year-old twin cousins, my sister's youngest children, Noah and Joshua. I say remarkable because Noah and Joshua are two of the most physically destructive human beings I've ever witnessed outside of adventure stories about cannibals. They are rowdy and rough and like to smash objects with their faces, and because you are none of those things, your father and I were worried that we might need to talk to my sister and make sure she didn't let them drop-kick you from the roof of their minivan.

But you transform them when you play with them, and they become these gentle, delicate creatures who want to show you the world. They argue over who gets to play with you next, often shoving the other one out of the way to be the one who gets to hold your hand. While we vacationed with my family over the recent Thanksgiving holiday, you spent almost every moment with those two, jumping on the bed or playing with flashlights or making tents. We thought you might be intimidated by their size and willingness to sacrifice their bodies to determine whether or not a surface can be dented, but just the opposite was true, and for three days I watched you bark orders: JUMP! GET DOWN! GET ME THAT! STOP CRYING! BRING ME THIS!

This month your fascination with purses has turned into a full-blown obsession, and sometimes when we leave the house you have to bring three or four of them with you, one around your neck, two hung over your right shoulder, one clutched in your hand. You also like to sleep with them, but that is not just limited to your purses. If I were to walk into your room right now and take a look inside your crib I'd find seven baby dolls, three Elmos, a Dr. Seuss book, a Dora book, four purses, a large pink ball, and a basket of bracelets. There is barely enough room for you to even sit upright in there. I decided long ago that I was not going to fight this battle, because I don't want to have to go rummaging around in the dark looking for a plastic baby when you wake up in the middle of the night and it's not tucked under your arm.

A few weeks ago, your father and I traded our queen-size bed for my father's larger king-size bed, one so massive it has its own area code, and in addition to saving our marriage, it has become your favorite place on Earth.

There are times when we cannot even pry you off of it, and to be honest, we usually don't want to. One of my favorite memories of your childhood will be the hours and hours we have spent as a family on this bed, your father and I sitting close together watching you perform somersaults or read books or sing along to Dora.

Last night after you ate a few crackers with peanut butter, your father fixed you a small bowl of ice cream, and when he set it in front of you, you glanced over it and then looked at me with very worried eyes. "Fix it, Mama," you said. I didn't know immediately what you were talking about, but when I looked at the ice cream sitting in perfectly round scoops in your bowl I instinctively took your spoon and began mushing it into a soft ice cream soup. And then I remembered for the first time in years, maybe a decade, that my father used to do the exact same thing for me. Ice cream tasted better after he had mushed it. I sat there for a second and smiled to myself in the warmth of that memory, and then later made a very important phone call to my father. I told him that I know he sometimes feels like he could have done better with me, but he should know he taught me many useful things that have made my life better. I hope to do the same for you.

Love,
Mama

Dear Leta,

Recently your father and I have discovered that we can resurrect old toys that you have long grown tired of by bringing them into our bed. Something about seeing them in that new landscape makes your head spin around, and the first time it happened we thought that it was going to short-circuit your brain. You were wanting your father to come into your room and play blocks, but we were watching something on the news, and because we were too lazy to pause the television he brought the blocks into our room and put them on the bed. You watched this happen, your head following him out of the room and then back in, and when he called you onto the bed you looked around to make sure he was talking to you. Like, Wait a minute. We're going to play blocks ON? THE? BED? WE CAN DO THAT? We had to convince you that this was perfectly okay, and once you climbed up and surveyed their scattered shapes across the mattress it was like you were seeing color for the first time. BLOCKS! ON THE BED! Who knew?

Now you play with all your toys on our bed, and every day sees a mass migration of plastic out of your room into ours. Purses and dolls and puzzles and every single book you own. You once asked to ride your tiny plastic bike on the bed, and although we did draw the line at that adventure, we do often let you drag up your new Elmo chair, a giant red throne that is twice your size. It has shared space in your bed on more than one night, taken rides with us to the grocery store, and has repeatedly been denied entry into the bathtub. Sometimes we put that chair up on the couch and you will sit in it between us while we all three read books, your father and I unable to see each other through the enormous red wall.

This year Christmas morning made more sense to you because you have been given many presents in the last several months, most of them from my mother, who cannot pass up an opportunity to show you how fulfilling a life full of jewelry can be. I think she may feel that she did something wrong with me, because how could it be that her own daughter doesn't regularly wear pearls? And she wants to right that wrong with you. She's doing a heck of a job, too, because you often wear more jewelry than I do. And when we're out together I sometimes think people are wondering how in the world you ever let your mother leave the house looking like *that*. And you're all, Yeah, I know.

One other thing you've suddenly started doing is this fake laugh that turns into a real laugh that turns into hysterical laughter. I have no idea where you learned it, but out of nowhere you'll start making this really low stuttering noise in the back of your throat that sounds very much like a car that won't start. And then pretty soon you're laughing so hard that your entire body is moving up and down. The sound is spectacular, and without fail it always makes us crack up. Last night while we were giving you a bath your father kept rolling his eyes and asking who tooted, and I didn't own up to it because it wasn't me. You kept shaking your head no until a giant bubble slipped out from underneath you and exploded so violently on the surface that it splashed the walls. You immediately looked at us like, Um, that wasn't me either. And then all three of us were laughing so hard that the walls seemed to be trembling under the echoes. Later on in your life, I think you'll look back and smile the most when you think about what it was like growing up in this house, the three of us laughing in chorus. And whether it be over a toot in the bathtub or because I've knocked my forehead into the door again, it doesn't matter, because the sound is the same, and that sound will always hold us together.

Love,
Mama

Dear Leta,

Happy Birthday! We had been telling you for a few weeks that your birthday was coming soon, and on Saturday morning when you woke up, I told you that it was finally here, that three years ago you came into this world. I then asked if you remembered how old you were, and you said, "Three, huh?" And when I smiled you added rather blankly, "I think that's pretty good. Three." As if you had come to terms, and it was something you could live with.

All day long you asked for birthday cake, because that is what a birthday signifies to you, and being the very mean mother that I am, I wouldn't let you eat any until after dinner. This didn't stop you from asking again and again, using several different variations on the question. At first you asked politely, even energetically, because you were certain that I would have to give in. But I said no, and that's when you started pleading. For what seemed like hours. Eventually you threw your body facedown across my lap and screamed CAAAAAAAAKE. It was just that important. And normally I would tell you to snap out of it, because there aren't many things in this world that are worthy of you making a fool out of yourself. It's just . . . chocolate cake happens to be one of those things.

Now when it's time to start the day, you act like you've already had your coffee. You get to wear a NEW SHIRT! A NEW LELLOW SHIRT! LOOK AT THAT SHIRT, MOM! WHAT A BEAUTIFUL SHIRT! And then after you brush your teeth WITH A NEW BRUSH! A DORA BRUSH! I LOVE THE DORA BRUSH! IT'S A GREAT BRUSH! It's time to take your vitamins, your NEW ORANGE VITAMINS! I LOVE THESE VITAMINS, MOM! THEY TASTE SO GOOD, THESE VITAMINS!

This is how you talk about things now: you declare what something is, describe its color, determine if it is old or new, and then make a final announcement about whether or not it is worth your time. It's a shirt, a blue shirt, a *new* blue shirt. You love this new blue shirt. It's a cup, a green cup, a not-new green cup. It's not great, the not-new green cup.

This month you've mastered the act of memorizing the books we read to you, and often you will read them back to us, not always word for word, but always understanding what is happening on each page. Sometimes when I'm lazy I'll try to skip whole sentences, and you always catch me and force me to go back and read it the right way.

As we all begin this new year together, I want you to know that the last year was the best we have had with you by far. I had been worried that this would be a tricky year, because legend has it that two-year-olds can be "terrible twos." I have known many two-year-olds in the past who had me convinced that I wanted to give birth to a full-grown thirty-year-old. So I had no idea it could be so marvelous, so full of off-key songs and belly laughs and racing each other down the cereal aisle. There have been so many moments that have made your father and me question whether life could get any fuller. You bring us closer when I see how much he loves you, how he looks at me when you do something funny so that we can share that brief moment together. Living with you has been something else we have fallen in love over, and even more than our favorite music or the sushi we like to eat when we go out, *you* are what we have in common. And every night after we put you to bed and settle down to watch a show or read a book, your father and I will first talk to each other in your voice, will repeat something funny you have said during the day, because we miss you already.

Love,
Mama

 112

MONTH THIRTY-SEVEN

Dear Leta,

I have been in bed for four days with the worst sinus infection I've had in years, and it's tough, tough work watching from the bed as your father takes care of everything. I can't remember the last time I was sick enough that I haven't been able to get up and dress you in the morning, which has always been one of my favorite parts of the day. I love putting you in your little denim pants and Converse high-tops, love parting your hair evenly into little curly ponytails. Your father normally does a terrible job dressing you, often pairing purple shirts with green pants and pink shoes. Remind me to tell you about what he was wearing the very first time I saw him, this will explain a lot. But these last few days he has really impressed me, and each morning he has dressed you in actual dresses, ones given to you by friends and family who are very worried about the high-tops. Dresses with ruffles. And bows. And because I am not a huge fan of little frilly dresses, this was an incredible novelty to you, and more than once you have twirled around the living room shouting I LOVE THIS CUTE DRESS!

This month you continue to delight us with your enthusiasm for life, and often your father and I have to check with each other to see if we have heard you correctly. One morning I told you we were going to the bank and you said, "I get it! The bank! That sounds like a great idea!" Generally you are this perky when we make plans to leave the house, often telling us that you love wherever it is that we're going, even if you haven't ever been there. Sometimes I'll push back and be all, Oh really? You love the dog food store? WHAT'S IT LIKE? And your eyes will get impossibly wide as you say something about it being really big, the big dog food store.

This month we re-enrolled you in a gym class, the same one we had you in about a year ago. Last week was your first class, and both your father and I tagged along to see how well you would take to the other kids and the program, and we were both so stunned with how much different you are, at least in terms of being willing to try things physically. A year ago you were still new to walking and had a hard time even taking a step off a two-inch gym mat by yourself. This time you ran to each different station ready to climb and tumble, albeit still very tenderly. Like last year, you were the most tentative kid there, the one who was much more interested in figuring out whether or not something had the mechanics to hold your weight before you trusted it with your life. One of the most distinctive memories I will have of you as a kid is the picture of you in the gym huddled over the joint in the balance beam, inspecting how the two pieces of wood fit together, while behind your head all these crazed, barefoot boys are flying horizontally through the air.

This month we also filled out an application for preschool, something we hope you'll get to start later this year, and late one night your father and I filled out several pages full of questions. We had to discuss several things, including what we hope you will get out of the program and which class we think would be right for you, and then we came back to the one question we saved for last: How would you describe your child's personality? And we didn't even know where to begin. It was one of the hardest questions I've ever been asked because there were only three lines for the answer, and I felt like I was trying to describe a rainbow to someone who has been blind their entire life. And I didn't know if they were trying to mess with all these parents, because I know I'm not the only one who sat there staring at that question thinking back over every moment I have lived with you, knowing that whoever gets to spend their days with you will be transformed by the experience, and that the only right answer would be: You will *not* be disappointed.

Love,
Mama

Dear Leta,

In a couple of weeks we're going to be moving into our new house, our NEW! BIG! HOUSE!, and you seem to be very excited about this, especially about your new big room and the new big "Play Park." Every time you have been in your new room you've thrown your arms wide and run in circles as if you could not believe that there was this much space anywhere in the world. The backyard seems to go on for miles, and this summer we're going to have a lot of fun back there swinging and blowing bubbles and watching Daddy throw the basketball at the hoop only to miss it by four feet.

Last week we got some great news about my brother. He is going to be moving his wife and four children down here from Seattle where they have been living for the last eight years, and for the first time in almost two decades my entire family will be living in the same city. This means that you've got four more cousins to boss around. And because our whole family is going to get to see so much more of each other, because you're going to get to grow up knowing his kids, I don't think I'd rather be anywhere else in the world right now. I feel like there is so much to look forward to, and I can say confidently that this is the best feeling in the world.

Love,
Mama

Dear Leta,

We did not realize that this house was going to be so good for you in so many ways, and have been thrilled to watch you climb up and down the stairs by yourself with increasing speed. Because you were so late to walk, you have also been a little late to other things, including jumping and running and climbing a set of stairs. We have forced you to walk the stairs by yourself several times a day thinking that it would increase the strength in your legs, and what do you know! Our instincts were right! This hasn't happened very often during our tenure as parents, that an instinct has turned out to be an actual instinct and not just severe heartburn.

I have been away on a vacation for the last several days, and while I was gone you were very good to your father and didn't complain too much. In fact, you slept in late every morning and then took long naps in the afternoon. When you and your father came to pick me up at the airport I was relieved that you were excited to see me. Your father had pulled your hair into a loose ponytail and dressed you in a pink summer dress, and your arms and legs were covered with yellow and green marker. I couldn't believe how much you had grown in the time I was away, it seemed like half a foot. We stood beside the baggage carousel hand-in-hand, and you kept looking up at me as if you couldn't believe it was me, while I kept leaning down to smell the top of your head, so thrilled that I was home. And then you started rubbing the back of my hand with your thumb, which is something I always do to you when I'm holding your hand to let you know that I am right here, that I have you and won't let you go. I like to think that the reason you rubbed me back was because you believe me.

Love,
Mama

MONTH FORTY

Dear Leta,

Just yesterday you started preschool. Yesterday morning I went over the major points with you again before we left and told you about all the books you'd get to read, about the playground with the swings, and the blocks and toys and crayons. You hung on every word, nodded vigorously at the thought of all those books, and when I asked you what you thought, you said, "And we'll get to watch TV, too, huh?"

Your first day went relatively well, and other than a rough transition when we dropped you off—a few tears, some spiderlike crawling up my legs—you had a great day, made a few friends, and got to play with what seemed like a million new toys. The highlight of your day, though, was when the teacher showed you the toilet, and it wasn't just an ordinary toilet. It was a Dora potty, with a cushiony Dora seat, and it had

Dora on it. With Dora. And when we picked you up you didn't want to leave without showing me the Dora potty, so I was all, Fine, let's have a look at this Dora potty. So we walked into the bathroom, and you ran right over to it, and before I could stop you, you hugged it.

A couple of weeks ago your father got it in his head that he wanted to potty train you, suddenly, without any preparation, even though you know and I know that you're just not ready yet. So I stood back and let him try it, watched from the sidelines as you refused over and over again to have anything to do with it. For two days straight he had you do nothing but sit on that potty, and you gleefully played along knowing that the moment he turned his back you were going to hop up onto the couch or bed and go to the bathroom there. And so he finally gave up and agreed to postpone his efforts for a few weeks, and I most certainly did not tell him that I told him so.

For the past week or so both you and I have been very sick with a cold, a fever, and an endless, hacking cough. While being sick is not ever any fun, it does allow me the very infrequent opportunity to sleep next to you, and one afternoon last week we both napped next to each other for a few hours on our bed. We both snored through our congested sinuses, and at one point you rolled over, grabbed my arm, and pulled it over so that my hand was cradling your face. And then you fell back asleep underneath my fingers. That was just, I don't know, exactly what anyone hopes being a parent is going to be.

Love,
Mama

Dear Leta,

I will look back on this month of your life as The Month of Cousin GEORGE! as you and he have become special buddies. At first I thought you weren't ever going to take to that kid, and for a few weeks you hated it when he even looked at you, but I noticed the change one afternoon during our first trip to the new Ikea when we left GEORGE! to look after our large purchases while we ran to get the car. When we backed out of the parking space you started screaming, "WE LEFT GEORGE! WE LEFT GEORGE!" and even after I assured you that we were going right then to pick him up, you tried to wrangle yourself out of your seat, presumably to get out of the car and find GEORGE! It wasn't until we met him at the loading zone and you saw him standing there that you calmed down, and that's when you took a deep breath and said, "I'm okay, I'm okay." As if watching out for him was your responsibility, and was that ever a close call.

He often likes to sit with you and watch entire episodes of Dora, and although he's probably not too proud to admit it, he can sing along to every song almost better than you. In fact, whenever Dora turns to the camera and asks the audience a question, GEORGE! always has a thoughtful answer.

A few days ago it was time for you to take a nap, but GEORGE! didn't know this and turned on another episode of Dora for you to watch. I walked in, paused the television, and said, no, not now, it's time for bed. Your lip quivered as you asked, please, could you watch more Dora, and I said again, not right now, maybe later. That's when you would normally turn to your father and start crying, but your father was in the other room. Only other person nearby was GEORGE!, and you were desperate, so you tried to get GEORGE! on your side, YOU ASKED HIM TO OVERRULE ME.

One, how cute is it that you reached out to him like that? That you thought him a close enough friend to back you up? Two, this shows that somewhere along the way you've learned a game of numbers, that two is stronger than one, and you're starting to realize that you have options.

For the last four weeks you've been going to preschool every morning, and although that first week was tough, you have since loved the idea of heading out every day to see your friends. I think preschool has been a fantastic addition to your life. Your teachers have sent home several drawings and projects you have done. They say you're getting along with the other kids, and that you've even agreed to play in the sand, which shows what magicians those people are. You've never liked sand, because it's *dirty*. And it *gets on things*.

They've also mentioned more than once that you're a great kid, that you're sweet and one of the most incredibly gentle kids they've ever met. And I know that when you read these letters you may not believe that you're this gentle little being, but there's no truer word to describe you. Gentle. I don't mention it nearly enough, but that is the impression you leave with people. You have a softness about you that almost startles people, because it's very different from the loud and often jarring movements of many kids your age. So I want you to know it, from me, the one who takes notes and writes about all your other faces, that I love your gentle one the most, and I know that it is the real you.

Love,
Mama

MONTH FORTY-TWO

Dear Leta,

Something happened this month, some switch was flipped. Suddenly we are parents of a kid who will not sit still, and this is uncomfortably new for us. You have always been a pretty low-energy child, and so our experience as parents has been markedly different from what most normal parents go through. Only recently have we really had to keep tabs on your whereabouts, and one of us will look up and suddenly notice you're not in the room, and the sensation is as startling as realizing we've left the oven on for a week.

Many parents have kids who start exploring like this within their first year, and so they spend years of their lives chasing after their children and searching for the ones who have suddenly disappeared. Like my sister, your aunt, whose twin boys both started walking at ten months, and since that day almost six years ago she hasn't once slept with both eyes closed. You have never been this type of kid. You were never one to explore electrical outlets or teeter over the edge of a stair-case. You've never climbed on top of a wobbly piece of furniture or tried to jump off a dresser. In fact, you still think that it's physically impossible to get out of your bed unless we come to get you.

Until this month.

On a recent trip to a clothing store, I was picking up some new shirts with a gift certificate my mom had given me for my birthday, and I wrongly assumed that your father was keeping an eye on you. Because suddenly I'm standing there trying to find an XL white T-shirt when I see that you are two steps from the front door of the store and are about to shoplift a pink bikini.

This is just not something that happens. You're never more than a step away from us in public, and that's only when you're not clinging to one of our legs or clutching monkeylike to my neck. You have magically broken free of some invisible wall that has been keeping you from exploring the world. And while this development is thrilling to watch, it's been a bit of an adjustment.

I'm certain that preschool has a lot to do with these changes, although I think I can safely blame preschool for a lot of things. Like your sudden interest in *SpongeBob SquarePants*. This morning during breakfast you suddenly set down your spoon and asked for a pop, a white pop, a white pop right now, please. And I had no idea what you were talking about, tried to clarify exactly what you were asking for, a popsicle? A can of soda? A single kernel of popcorn? And you continued to shake your head at every suggestion, so I asked you where this white pop is stored and you said, "I do not know this." Like, You're the mom, I thought *you* would know these types of things. And I never did figure out what a white pop was.

I also think that you're holding yourself together pretty well in school, and then when we come to pick you up and you see the two of us, it's all you can do to make it to the door without losing your mind. Your teacher says you're terrific in class, never a complaint, but when we get into the car you're all, *Do you know how hard it is to be this terrific?* The rides home from school are never much fun because you're so incredibly grumpy from having kept it together for four hours. I know you act that way around us because we are your parents. This was the exact dynamic I had with my mother my entire childhood, and I can remember many instances when the mere sight of her face would make me crumble into a sobbing pile of mush because I had been needing to let go like that, and she was the only one I could trust with the privacy of that emotion.

Sometimes you have really bad days and you need to cry about it, and I'm glad that you love us enough to do it in front of us. I know that sounds strange, but that's what love is, being able to confide in someone that everything isn't okay, and trusting that they will listen.

Love,
Mama

Dear Leta,

This month you have taken serious interest in the dog for the first time. You've suddenly started asking about Chuck when you wake up in the morning, as if you cannot start your day until you know where he is. When I say, You know, I have no idea where that dog is, you will call out for him—CHUUUUUUUCK!— and continue doing so until he reluctantly crawls into the room. You've also been playing games of chase with him, and last night when you caught up with him you started to throw your leg over his back for "a fun pony ride," but I stopped you. One, that would hurt the dog, obviously. Two, the look on his face was, This? THIS IS NOT FUN FOR ME.

Month forty-three was also the month when you officially dropped your nap. For good. There is no more napping. Some days I still make you take some down-time, and you and I will go down to our big bed together and lie there quietly for an hour, but even that quiet time is becoming a nuisance. I'll lie there with my eyes closed while you tap my forehead with your index finger, an indication of the fact that YOU. ARE. NOT. TIRED. And then it's, Can I have some water? Where's my pillow? Where's Chuck? Why is it dark in here? Why is Daddy upstairs? Why is the blanket this color? Why does the fan go so fast? Why is the window over there?

You've also started saying "honey" quite frequently, as a go-to word whenever there's silence, except you say it like "hun-ehhhhhh," like you're out of your mind. We couldn't figure out where you picked it up, and then we learned that there are two sisters in your class at school, and the younger one calls the older one honey. You know that you're being funny when you say it, and you've even started to pronounce other words this way: mommy is mum-ehhhhhh, daddy is dud-ehhhhhh, puppy is puh-pehhhhhh. Out of nowhere you'll say one of these words, like we'll be driving to school and without any context whatsoever you'll suddenly go HUN-EHHHHHHH! Or you'll wake up in the morning and call out to me from your room, MUM-EHHHHHHH! Followed by hysterical laughter. And I know you're in there smiling to yourself, like, *These people have no idea how lucky they are to have me in their lives*.

And the thing is, you won't say hun-ehhhhhh for anyone else. You only do it in front of me and your father. Earlier this week I asked Grandmommy if she had heard you say it during the time that you were staying with her while we were in Los Angeles. And she had no idea what I was talking about. *Honey? What?* And for a second I was worried that maybe you'd decided that you were over it, that honey was like, so seven days ago. But the moment Grandmommy left and you were alone with us for the first time in five days, you held out your arms in a welcoming gesture and shouted MUM-EHHHHHHH! DUD-EHHHHHHH! Our little inside joke. Leta, we know *exactly* how lucky we are to have you in our lives.

Love,
Mama

Dear Leta,

One morning early this month you woke up, took a look around your bed, and suddenly realized that it was not, in fact, barricaded by an electrically charged barbwire fence. And I guess you were overcome by the enormous fortune of that, maybe you sat there for a few minutes figuring out the mathematics of what it meant, and then *you got out of bed without calling for us first*. This has never happened before, not once, and thinking that I was hearing the pitter-patter of the dog's paws on the carpet as he came to greet us that morning, I turned over in bed only to be greeted by your very white, very human face.

That particular discovery plus several nights spent in a strange hotel in San Francisco have turned you into a bit of a midnight roamer, and there hasn't been a single night in the last three weeks that we haven't had to get up and walk you back to your bed, three or four times a night. You're always complaining about how dark it is, or how you need a drink of water, or how it's cold in your room, always searching for some excuse to be up and out of your room at three o'clock in the morning.

So something happened this month, and all of a sudden you're obsessed with gory things. Weird gory things, like crushed insects and bleeding wounds. If either your father or I stub our toe or cut our finger, your first response is not, Hey there, are you okay? It's I WANNA SEE, and you won't let us bandage the wound until you have thoroughly inspected it and determined that it is, indeed, very gross. The other night when I was changing into my pajamas in our closet, trying to hurry so that your father wouldn't see my half-naked body tucked behind the wall of hanging belts and think PARTY IN THE CLOSET, you were clinging to my leg, barraging me with questions, pointing to the tiny alcove at the back of the closet we use to store Christmas decorations, and I stupidly told you, no, you can't go in there because of all the spiders on the floor. I might as well have said BEHIND THAT CURTAIN ARE A MILLION M&M'S. Because you will not stop talking about the spiders, Can you see them? Can you see them now? Is there an appointment book where I can schedule you in to see them?

Recently your obsession with junk has become almost unmanageable, and on any given day our living room looks like a landfill. You collect everything—straws, napkins, junk mail, bubble gum wrappers—and many times I have sat down on the couch only to hear something crunch underneath my butt. And there behind the cushion is a piece of paper I had thrown away several days earlier. You call it "my stuff," and you like to take piles of it and shove it into various purses given to you by my mother. I'm not even lying, you've got thirty or forty different purses filled with trash, all of them scattered in different corners of the house, and the worst part about it is you remember *exactly* what trash is in which purse.

Preschool could not be going better, although there are mornings when I have to dissuade you from packing some of "your stuff" into the school bag. I think your teacher really likes you, because she's always got a story for us when we come to pick you up. Just today she looked up from a group of kids to say hello to you in the morning, and when you waved hello back to her she told us that you are always polite, always saying thank you and asking please in the right circumstances, always eager to share and acknowledge her when she asks you to do something. This is great news, because your father and I have worked very hard to teach you these manners, and we think that one of the most important things you can carry with you in your life is the ability to recognize that you're sharing the Earth with other people. It's something my parents were careful to teach me, and my father always made sure to show me how to give up a seat on the bus for someone who needs it more, or to look a stranger in the eye and ask them how their day is going.

Sometimes our days are really, really hard, like that one time you lost that Cheerio, remember that? Your father and I will not ever forget that, and that night like most other nights we lay in bed laughing until we cried about how you stood there screaming as Chuck licked it off the floor. This is life with a three-year-old, the kicking and screaming, the tackling and falling to pieces, all of it. It is a thrilling, exhausting ride with the most vibrant human being I've ever known, and my memories of this time are so colorful, so vivid and full of texture. My only sadness is that your memories of this time will not be as clear, so I want you to know that here, now, after a day of tripping over piles of sacred trash you have left in the middle of the floor, the three of us together, we're having a blast.

Love,
Mama

Dear Leta,

You have been sleeping with a Fisher-Price tape deck for the past week. Considering the vast array of ridiculous objects you have slept with in your life, this one doesn't seem that odd. Except that it's this gigantic piece of obsolete machinery, about half the size of your body, and during the day as you carry it around the weight of it is constantly pulling you to the ground. And yet, you will not leave it behind. You must have this cassette player with you at all times, so you'll walk into the room dragging this awkward mechanical behemoth behind you.

Since I once made my family leave a campsite because there were bugs there, it's not too surprising that you are still talking about an ant you saw in your room two weeks ago. You're still making me promise that the ant will not get you, and after breakfast in the morning as we're walking downstairs to your bedroom, you'll tug on my hand and say no, again, We can't go down there, there is an ant, and it is waiting behind that door. It is in cahoots with the moth that hovered outside the window last night as we ate dinner. Our only defense? To panic.

About a week ago you and I were sitting on the couch reading books together when you suddenly looked up at me and said, "We'll have a baby soon, huh?" And I really didn't know what to say. I don't know how much you understand about what has happened, that no, the baby we had talked about is no longer going to be coming to live with us. But I didn't want to confuse you any more than you already are about the whole thing, because for all you know babies suddenly show up on the porch in a box marked AMAZON.COM. It's just that the weirdest thing about this whole grieving process has been how much hope it has given me, how it has made everything clear to me about who I am and what I want, and I know that having lived through this we will somehow make it happen. So instead of saying anything to you, I just nodded my head and wiped my tears.

Love,
Mama

Dear Leta,

Seems we're having trouble communicating to you the whole idea of Santa Claus, because every time I bring him up and try to celebrate the fact that he brings presents, you start looking around for places to hide your garbage, *so he won't be tempted to steal it when he breaks in to our house*. I know when I'm covertly leaving presents under the tree in someone's living room, I'm also looking out for empty pudding containers I can grab before flying back up the chimney.

I will remember this last month as a phase when everything revolved around being poopy. It has become your favorite noun, your favorite verb, your favorite exclamation. Sometimes you will shout it in the middle of dinner, sometimes you will read a book and for ten pages it's all poopy, poopy, poopy, poopy? poopy, POOPY! poopy, poopy, poopy, The End. I'll ask you to spell your name and you'll scream POOPY! This gets old, yes, but it's a sign that you're very normal.

This has also been the month of bargaining, of seeing just how low you can get us to go on the price. When I've told you that you can't have a treat your response is, "Can I have a treat *soon*? How about a treat *in a minute*?" This back-and-forth happens all day long, over every single decision that is made, from what we put in your lunch to how many stories we read before bedtime. Can you have this soon? What about later? How about tomorrow? And when I say no, not tomorrow, not even the day after tomorrow, you're all, *What about the day after that one?* It doesn't stop until I agree to give in at a specified time in the future, until I have given you hope of it ever happening. So I'll finally cave and say, Fine. You can have a cookie in twenty years.

Over the last few weeks your love for Dora has been slowly replaced with a raging passion for princesses, specifically Ariel the mermaid, and if you aren't stroking her silky orange mane you're saying every line out loud as you watch the movie. You also love to sing the songs, love to sing *any* song for that matter, even though you haven't developed a sense of tone. There is one particular song in the mermaid movie where she's singing *ah-ah-ahhhh* up a string of notes, down a string of notes, and then back again as the evil squid witch steals her voice. I remember the first time I heard you singing along, it was this dead-sounding EHHHHHHHHHH, like a sick cow had fallen over in the mud.

I stopped whatever I was doing in the kitchen to listen more intently, to see if maybe I needed to run in and make sure you hadn't broken a limb, and as the song grew louder, so did your forlorn accompaniment until the entire house was filled with the sound of your voice. I couldn't see your face but knew you probably had your hands above your head and were feeling it every bit as much as that mermaid. It didn't matter that you weren't anywhere near the right key; that raucous, bellowing note electrified every nerve in my body.

Love,
Mama

Dear Leta,

We've spent many hours at the doctor's office over the last few weeks, including a few hours yesterday. You've been suffering from a cough for more than a month that at first was nothing to be alarmed about. You didn't have any other symptoms, no runny nose or fever, so we waited to take you to the doctor until the cough became more pronounced. He took a look at you, ordered some x-rays of your chest, and we walked over to the radiology department, where they strapped you into a protective gown and stood you in front of a large machine. I couldn't be in the room with you because there was a 2 percent chance that I might have been pregnant (turns out I wasn't), so you had to stand there . . . alone.

I should have had more faith in you that day, because they were able to take three x-rays and you cooperated like a perfect patient. I could not believe it, really, could not comprehend it as I stood there and watched through a window as the technician moved your body and you gladly acquiesced. You only showed a little bit of trepidation when you looked over to my face through the glass and started repeating, "I. AM. DOING. THIS." in a quiet voice.

Christmas this year with you was more enjoyable than it has ever been, even though you never did quite take to the idea of Santa Claus. In fact, on Christmas morning we had a hard time getting you to go upstairs to the living room because you thought Santa Claus was going to be there sitting on our couch. Once we convinced you that he had come and gone, that he was thousands of miles away, you cautiously tiptoed toward the mountain of presents, looked up at us in disbelief, and asked, "Are all those presents *my* presents?" Like, *This* is why everyone is so excited about this holiday? NO WONDER. And then every day for the next week you woke up and asked, "Is it Christmas today?"

This month we also got a new puppy, and I had no idea it would upset you so badly. It's obvious that you are very jealous of her, and when you see me cradling her in my arms you're quick to push her away and make sure that I still love you. The truth is, I am very much in love with the new puppy, wild about her, even. But that doesn't mean anything about the way I feel about you, and no pet would ever muddle the fact that you are my firstborn. Not even another child could come between me and you, and even though your father and I are actively looking forward to the possibility of another one, it's not because we're looking for something else. More than anything, you have made us more capable of loving, have made our hearts bigger by taking them from us, and my love for other people and animals, it's all there because I want to share the way you make me feel.

Love,
Mama

Dear Leta,

You are now four years old. To celebrate we gathered all the aunts, uncles, and cousins on my side of the family to eat pizza and birthday cake.

This last month, we took a trip to San Diego. Your father booked us into a pet-friendly hotel on the beach, and although I wasn't expecting the walls to be lined with gold leaf, I certainly didn't think I'd walk into that room and be smothered with the smell of urine. That was the scariest hotel room I've ever been in, and I was afraid to touch any surface for fear that I'd catch a deadly disease. This didn't stop you from running right in and throwing yourself headfirst onto the couch, a piece of furniture covered in mysterious stains, and shouting, "Are we here to play princesses?" That was so refreshingly innocent of you.

We ended up driving to a different, much nicer hotel the following day, and you were just as excited to stay there as you were at the dumpy one. That night we ordered room service, and the cart they wheeled our meal in on was so fancy you declared, "This is so lovely!"

Just yesterday, I read a woman's story of her son who died when he was very young, how she feels that he had chosen her as a mother before he was born because she was the one best suited to take care of his specific needs before he died. I'm not a very spiritual or religious person, but her story got me thinking that you were sent to me for very specific reasons, that something inside me is supposed to be called upon in regard to who you are as a person. It's a comforting thought that maybe you knew before I did that you'd really need me. So just in case, I want you to know that I'm honored you had so much faith that I was up to the task.

Love,
Mama

Dear Leta,

For a few weeks in the last month you had us very worried that no one in the house would ever get a full night's sleep again. Something repeatedly woke you up in the middle of the night and over and over again you'd show up in our room at two o'clock ready to watch television. Because your father and I were so tired we'd let you climb in bed with us, and then you'd spend the next six hours kicking us in the head. I'm not going to complain too loudly about the way you sleep because you inherited it directly from me, and my brother and sister like to tell and retell the story about how if faced with a decision between sharing a bed with me or sleeping on the couch, they chose to sleep outside in the garage because that was the only place far enough away that my elbows wouldn't jab them in the eyes.

So you've developed a certain way of speaking about things when you do not know the name of some-

thing, and instead of asking us to help you identify it you will simply refer to it by its color. One morning when you couldn't find THE GREEN! THE GREEN! WHERE IS THE GREEN! I looked at your father with a hopeful gaze that said, Please tell me you know what she's talking about. Except he was giving me the same look, and so we went searching for something green, but do you know how hard that is? There are a lot of green things in this house, and when we asked you to elaborate a little bit on the characteristics of The Green you said GREEEEEEN! IT'S GREEEEEEEN! WITH GREEEEEEN ON IT!

Eventually we found a green washcloth tucked underneath your pillow where you had slept with it next to your head, but this search has become so commonplace—we've done a hunt for The Yellow, The Red, and The Black all within the last week—that your father and I have started to speak to each other exactly like this. So I'll ask your father where he put The Blue, and he's all What? And I'm all, THE BLUE! THE BLUUUUUEEE! And he'll go, Oh yeah! The Blue! I put it on the thing over by the yellow.

Last night I had to go back into your room six or seven times so that you could ask me another question, could you eat Trix when you woke up? Could you watch *Cinderella* tomorrow? Could you take your new book to school and show it to your friends? And I was getting really impatient, and at one point I swung open your door and before you could say anything I yelled YES YOU CAN HAVE PRINCESS FRUIT SNACKS IN YOUR LUNCH TOMORROW, NOW GO TO SLEEP because that was the next question in the script. And you sat there silent on your bed for two or three seconds before saying, "But I just wanted to tell you that I love you." Which was your gentle way of saying, Hey, you need to calm down.

So I walked from the door to the side of your bed, kneeled down, and kissed you on your warm forehead. "I love you, too," I said.

You grabbed my hand and hugged it with both arms. "Mom," you whispered, your mouth close to my cheek, "can I have princess fruit snacks in my lunch tomorrow?"

Love,
Mama

Dear Leta,

Tomorrow you turn fifty-one months old. If you are reading these in chronological order you will probably notice that the newsletter for month fifty has gone missing. Yeah, about that. Would you believe me if I told you Coco ate it? You'd have to because Coco eats everything. Just this week she ate both the arms and legs off the new Barbie doll that my mother gave you, and when I found her chewing those limbs I secretly hoped you wouldn't notice. But that's not what happened at all. You noticed immediately and after several hours of wailing and head-butting the floor you walked up to me, put the legless and armless nub into my hands, and said, "Grandmommy is going to be so mad at that dog." And you used a tone that suggested it was less of an observation and more of a warning.

Fifteen years from now you're going to read this paragraph, here where I tell you that your favorite thing to say is DONKEY BELLIES, and whenever you say knock-knock, and I say who's there, you scream DONKEY BELLIES and then you gasp for air as the giggles get lodged in your throat, you're going to read this and then call me and go THERE'S NOTHING FUNNY ABOUT DONKEY BELLIES. And then you're going to ask me for money.

Love,
Mama

Dear Leta,

Tomorrow you turn fifty-two months old. It's a number you can easily count to, although recently counting things has become much too boring to hold your interest. You're so over it now, you go, "One, two, three . . . blah blah blah . . . one hundred."

For months you have begged us to go outside and blow bubbles and swim, and we've said we had to wait until all the snow melted. And for months you would wake up in the morning, look hopefully out your bedroom window, and ask Today? Has all the snow melted today? And I had to say, no, not today.

Well, the snow finally melted, and we have been swimming and blowing bubbles like mad, and the change in your mood has been so exaggerated. You seem much more invigorated by life, much more inspired to create stories and tell wild, imaginative tales. Your favorite stories are silly stories, all of them of course involving some form of donkey belly, bonkey delly, dookey boppy, or poopy smelly. At night after we read you a book or two you want us to lie with you for a few minutes before you sleep and tell you a silly tale. I'm not as good as Daddy is at this activity, because he was once a thirteen-year-old boy, and I don't have that kind of experience. But you love it when I talk about pink apples (!) or purple bananas (!!) or orange limes (!!!), because HOW SILLY IS THAT? Quite, apparently. One night we were both laughing so hard that your father asked what we'd been doing in there, he could hear us all the way across the house. And I was all, PURPLE BANANA, GET IT? And he was all, Excuse me? And I was all OBVIOUSLY YOU HAD TO BE THERE.

You still love to tell stories about princesses, and I get the feeling that your princess obsession has only just begun. It's recently become so intense that you refuse to wear anything but a dress and will not let me pull your hair out of your face "because Sleeping Beauty doesn't wear her hair that way."

Last week you spent several days with my mother while your father and I took a trip to Canada, and when we returned you were happier to see us than you've ever been. My mother reports that you were nothing but polite and delightful the entire time we were gone, and you remained that way for, oh, an hour. Right up until we got into the car to go pick up the dogs. Something switched and you cried about how Coco was going to eat your toys and you did not want Coco to eat your toys, but she was going to eat your toys AND IT WOULD MAKE YOU SAD! SAAADDDDDDD! I kept reassuring you that we would not let Coco eat your toys, but COCO! SHE WAS GOING TO EAT YOUR TOOOOOOOYYYYSS!

You were inconsolable, and whenever I am in a similar state all I want your father to do is shut up and listen to me. His instinct is to fix it, and that's not at all what I want. I don't want him to open the jar of pickles. I want him to understand HOW FRUSTRATED I AM THAT I CANNOT DO IT MYSELF, and then he needs to let me enumerate every other issue that the jar of pickles is bringing to the surface. Your fear of Coco eating your toys represents something larger, other fears, perhaps the perception that we don't take Your Stuff seriously enough, or maybe you think she gets more attention than you do. Whatever the case, I really listened to what you were saying. As family we owe each other that. I let you wail about how you'd never be able to sleep again because Coco eating your stuff was making you too tired to sleep (I am not even kidding, you actually said that), and then let you work through your emotions like I try to do, like your father always waits for me to do. And when we got home you stiffened your upper lip, took one stern look at that dog, and said, "Don't even think about it."

Love,
Mama

MONTH FIFTY-THREE

Dear Leta,

One morning I walked into your room when it was time to get up, told you good morning, and then headed to your window to open your shades. You sat straight up in bed and said, "Do you have something to say to me?" Now, that is something a woman says to her husband when he comes home late smelling of someone else's perfume, and since I didn't remember participating in anything so scandalous, I just shook my head and continued going about the morning ritual. But you were adamant and repeated that question emphatically several times until you'd had enough and screamed DID YOU SLEEP OKAY! DID YOU SLEEP OKAY! DID YOU SLEEEEEEEEEP OKAAAAAAAAAAY! So I paused, asked you if you had slept okay, and you said, "Why, yes, thank you very much."

Earlier this month we took a vacation to Florida, and the trip there was the longest day of travel-

ing we've ever attempted with you. Surprisingly you held up quite well through both plane rides and the two-hour drive to our condo, and the only time we thought you were going to lose it was on the descent of the second flight into Mobile, Alabama. The pressure in the cabin started messing with your ears, and at one point you started yelling, "I DON'T HAVE A VOICE!"

We spent seven days in Florida, and although we tried to get you to enjoy the beach you would not put your feet down and touch the sand. If there is one unassailable truth that we keep butting up against as your parents it's that you will try something new only when you are good and ready. This has been true of every milestone in your short four years here, from sitting up to crawling to walking, from eating and sleeping to meeting new people. Our instinct as parents is to panic and try to fix the problem when in reality there is no problem. You are just taking your time. And really, all you want from us is to give you that time.

On the last night of our vacation we were out getting dinner at a restaurant on the beach when suddenly I looked up and saw you running after the two kids who had been with us all week. On the beach. In the sand. WITHOUT SHOES. All of us just sat there in silence and stared. I know it sounds weird to say that I was proud of you for walking on the beach, but there it is, I WAS SO PROUD. That moment was just a continuation of so many other moments when you were saying to us, Hey, everything is fine, I'm just deciding for myself when I'm ready. And right now I'm ready.

Love,
Mama

Dear Leta,

A couple of days ago you turned fifty-four months old. I'm sure that if you were sitting here right now and I told you this you'd ask me why. And I'd say because when you add up all the months you've been alive it totals fifty-four. And then you'd go, why? And I'd say, because that's how math works. And you'd go, but why?

This month the list of words you can read has multiplied quite a bit, and often you're spelling words out loud at random times. Like, Oooh, look, there's a cat. C-A-T. Or, I love you, Mom. M-O-M. We bought you a book filled with Disney princesses that is designed to help kids your age learn to read, and within a few days you had memorized the whole thing and were reciting it back to me. Your teacher had seen you doing this with that book at school and she pulled me aside one day to congratulate me on your reading skills. And I was all, Um, Leta memorized that book as I read it to her. I don't think there's much reading going on. She shook her head and said, "That's exactly what reading is."

A couple of weeks ago Utah celebrated Pioneer Day. It's a huge holiday here, almost bigger than the Fourth of July, and because we had some old fireworks in the basement we decided to join in the festivities. You and I were sitting in the driveway as Daddy lit sparklers on the street, and suddenly you peeked through the sleeve in my shirt, pointed at the stubble of hair on my underarm, and shrieked, "BLEEEEEAHHHHH!" I asked you what could possibly be so wrong that you would go and imitate a goat and you responded, "BLEEEEEAHHHHH!" I told you that one day you, too, would grow hair on your underarms, and you protested for several minutes that you were not ever going to get big, not if it meant having BLEEEEEAHHHHH! on your arms.

And then your father set off a firework that was a little too loud for your taste, and you could not hop off that driveway fast enough. We'd shut the door tightly to keep the hot evening air from entering the house, and because you couldn't open it yourself you sat down on the stoop, covered your ears, and started shouting I WANT TO GO INSIDE AND READ BOOKS. I WANT TO GO INSIDE AND READ BOOKS. Your father and I looked at each other knowingly. We understand you, have watched you, and learned your limits. Sometimes members of our extended family will try to push things with you even after I have said, Please, hear me out, I know my daughter and what you're doing is not going to work. And they'll continue to push all the while you continue to show them that regardless of how hard they shove you, you will not budge. Sure, sometimes you need to be pushed, but sometimes what you need most is an advocate. And I want you to know that when you need me I will be your greatest champion. So together we went inside and read books.

Love,
Mama

Dear Leta,

I don't know if I'm ever going to be able to convince you to wear pants again. You haven't worn a pair of pants in over three months because of all your summer dresses, and believe me, I think it should be legal to walk around without pants on, I would sign that petition and vote for the person who would pass that legislation, but sometimes it's just not practical.

Last week my half of the family wanted to get together at a local park to celebrate Labor Day, and I made the huge mistake of telling you about it without first checking to make sure that nothing was going to disrupt those plans. So I told you about the park and that's all you talked about for two days, and then that Monday morning it was pouring down rain and the temperature had dropped almost thirty degrees. Plans changed and now we were going to meet at Papaw's house, and when I told you about that minor adjustment, explained the change in weather, you went all BUT I WANTED TO GO TO THE PAAAARRRRK! And I was all, Really? I never would have guessed that. And you were all, BUT WE CAN PUT ON A JACKET AND GO TO THE PAAAARRRRK! So I said, Look, we can go to the park, but you're going to have to put on pants. You blinked very rapidly for about ten seconds, in silence, and then said, "I think we better go to Papaw's."

Love,
Mama

Dear Leta,

This month we've seen a huge change in your physical development, and once where you were tentative about jumping or climbing you're now aggressively curious. Last week you climbed the rock wall on the swing set in the backyard for the first time, just hopped right onto it, seized one of the grips, and starting pulling yourself up. Both your father and I looked at each other like, When did you teach her how to do that? And then immediately realized this was something you thought up by yourself.

Your hand-eye coordination has also seen some improvement, at least enough that your father will now let you play Super Mario Galaxy with him. Last week I had to give a lecture and left your father in charge of putting you to bed. That's nothing out of the ordinary, but when I got home an hour and a half after your bedtime, your father was standing at the door nearly out of breath. I asked him what was wrong, and he goes, Oh this? And then he explains that you guys had lost track of time playing Super Mario Galaxy, and you are really good at it now, and with you on his team he's able to advance farther than he ever has! You could see the possibilities going off like bombs behind his eyes.

A few weeks ago I started a new routine with you when I put you to bed. After we read books I now talk to you about your day instead of telling princess stories, and at first you were really resistant to this idea because it didn't seem reasonable. Hadn't I seen what you'd done during the day? Why do we now have to *talk* about it? But you soon warmed to the idea, and now we talk at length about every little detail of your life: what you had for breakfast, the outfit you wore, what games you played at school, which friend has a new Dora bike, the game of hide-and-seek we played before dinner. At this point in the routine I've turned off the light and I'm lying next to you as you recount your day, and most of the time you're accidentally hitting me in the face as you swing your arms wide to show JUST. HOW. MUCH. you loved that game of hide-and-seek. I guess you could say I started this routine with the hope that we could continue to talk this way throughout your life, or that at least it wouldn't be foreign to you to share such details with me later on. Maybe this is my way of letting you know as early as I

can that this is the type of relationship I want to culti-
vate with you, and that I will always be interested in
the highs and lows, the exciting and the mundane, all
of it. You will always be one of the most interesting
people in the world to me.

Love,
Mama

Dear Leta,

Last week for Halloween you dressed up as your favorite princess, Sleeping Beauty, and went trick-or-treating with all ten of your cousins on my side of the family. You had been undecided for quite some time concerning your costume, and every day it changed from Sleeping Beauty to Jasmine and then back to Sleeping Beauty, but you were always certain that you wanted Daddy to dress up as your prince, and me? You wanted me to dress up as a witch.

This year since you were much more familiar with the concept of Halloween, you were less impressed that strangers were passing out candy and much more interested in when we could go home and eat it. Like, maybe after the first house. The second that first person dropped two miniature candy bars into your bag you whipped around and asked if we could head back and eat them *now*. Not yet, we said, how about we gather more treats, and this made sense to you, at least up until the second house when again you asked if we could be done. Somehow you lasted a good half hour, and when we finally called it a night and headed home I could tell that you were totally sweating it. Was I going to let you eat your treats? You didn't know, and you couldn't look me in the eye, so you asked your prince, who in turn told you to ask the witch. HA HA!

I said yes. Of course. It's Halloween. And Leta, I don't think you have ever loved me more than you did in that moment. In fact, you took the time to hug me and tell me that I am wonderful before ripping into a full-sized Hershey bar. It is not lost on me that you showed such affection because of a chocolate bar and not because I carried you in my womb for nine months or cupped my hands underneath your mouth when you threw up a cheese quesadilla.

Love,
Mama

Dear Leta,

Earlier this month we spent several days with your father's side of the family at a cabin in northern Utah for Thanksgiving, and it marked the first time we've ever taken a vacation where you were not totally freaked out about the change. In fact, the change energized you, and for three straight days you played with your nine-year-old cousin, occasionally coming downstairs to announce that you loved it there and were never leaving. You loved it so much, in fact, that you barely noticed the large number of strange people coming and going. You even interacted with people you had never met before, *STRANGERS*, something I didn't expect to happen for several decades.

The night before we left when I tried to prepare you for the fact that we were leaving the next morning, you started bawling into your bowl of Cinnamon Toast Crunch, something you had eaten at every single meal. So I tried to cheer you up by mentioning the fact that we were driving to Grandmommy's house the next day, and your countenance changed immediately. You asked if we were staying there "for a lot of nights," and jokingly I threatened to leave you there forever. "FOREVER?" you asked, and just as I was about to assure you that I was only kidding you dropped your spoon, wiggled your fingers in the air, and shouted, "I WOULD LOVE TO STAY THERE FOREVER!"

The past month has been dominated with the idea of the new baby, and in trying to describe the time line of events your father momentarily lost his brain and told you that the baby would be here when the snow melted. Such an explanation would hold up if this winter were exactly like the last one when we didn't see actual patches of grass until May, but already we've had snow come and go, and that baby isn't here yet. So when your father picked you up from school today your first question was, "Is Mom's baby out?" And when he answered no you were quick to point out that the snow had melted. So here, since your father isn't the one throwing up twice a day and will never know what it's like to feel his thighs unhinge and move in opposite directions, let me clear it up for you: ETERNITY. THAT'S HOW LONG THE BABY WILL BE IN MY TUMMY.

Several times in the last few weeks you have pointed toward your own full stomach and announced that you're having a girl, an excruciatingly adorable habit that turned sour once you started pointing to overweight people in public and wondering out loud about the sex of their babies.

I have to say that going through this experience with you as a four-year-old could not possibly be more enjoyable. I love your curiosity and concern, your anticipation, how you repeatedly assure me that when the baby gets here you will totally share your nachos with her. And I refer to the baby as "her" because you will not even consider the alternative, and there are times when I bring up the possibility and you will hold up your hand to silence me, as if I'm talking about something appalling.

Mostly, I am excited that this baby will have you as an older sister, and not just because you will both need someone to call to complain about the fact that your parents are nuts. Sure, there will be times when you'll both try to kill each other, either through physical brutality or embarrassment, but I know that at some point this baby is going to look up to you and think you are the coolest thing that ever walked on the planet. And while there is no way to predict the lasting dynamic of a relationship between siblings, I can only hope that you will have with this one what I have with my own, a bond so strong that it doesn't even matter that we have nothing but our parents in common. They are lifelines, people who were there, who were witnesses to everything that made me who I am, and I am the same for them in return. Is the relationship perfect? No, but we all know that we would sacrifice anything for each other, and one of the many reasons your father and I decided to have another child was to give you the possibility of that friendship.

Love,
Mama

MONTH SIXTY

Dear Leta,

Yesterday you turned five years old, or you could say that you celebrated your sixtieth month of life. Turns out I didn't write a newsletter for your fifty-ninth month, and I blame that entirely on what I call placenta brain, the situation that occurs when a pregnant woman's blood supply is so concentrated on growing someone else's fingers and toes that her brain doesn't have enough juice to complete simple tasks. Like remembering her husband's name. Or turning off the car before going inside the grocery store.

I cannot wrap my head around the idea that you've been in our lives for five years, that seems impossible, wasn't it just yesterday that they yanked you out of my womb and placed you trembling onto my exhausted chest? I come back to that memory of you often, your right arm extended toward my face, the two of us meeting for the first time. I remember thinking, OH MY GOD I GAVE BIRTH TO MY HUSBAND.

You looked exactly like him, still do, and sometimes in the mornings I will roll over in bed and see you nestled into his arm watching cartoons, and in the darkness of those early hours your profiles are such that I have to strain to detect who is who. Since I've been pregnant he has taken over most of the morning responsibilities, and that includes making room for you on his side of the bed when you show up before seven o'clock. You are now conditioned to walk over to his side of the room, reach out your arms, and ask, "Is it time for SpongeBob?" And then for the next hour I will nod in and out of sleep to the sound of you two laughing and making fart noises with your hands.

Your fifth year was by far the best yet, and not just because you are almost totally self-sufficient, although that does help quite a bit. There came a point in the last year when we felt like we were home free, like Well, she can dress herself, pour her own cereal, and read instructions, what's left for us to do? And now that you've got Wikipedia, do you really need two aging and out-of-touch busybodies trying to guide you through life? I'm thinking we're needed from here on out for the sole purpose of driving you to and from birthday parties.

One of the biggest developments in the last year has been your love of reading, and the fact that you caught on so fast will forever amaze us. We've fostered this skill here and there but never expected you to take to it so quickly. You're reading everything now: head-lines, boxes of crackers, the publisher information on the inside jacket of every book. Every night you read us a bedtime story, sometimes stumbling through three-syllable words but always embracing victory when you sound out something correctly. This is a bit-tersweet development, as now your father and I can no longer spell things out around you when we don't want you to know what we're talking about.

Your father and I have been making a special effort these last few months to savor this time we have with you alone, time before all our lives are disrupted by the arrival of a new family member. I remember during that first year with you spending Saturday mornings in our bedroom watching marathon episodes of *Queer Eye for the Straight Guy*, how you'd kick your feet the moment you recognized the theme song. I remember when you were eighteen months old, how you'd repeat the word LEEGO from the backseat when you were tired of riding around in the car. I remember chasing you up and down the aisle at the grocery store when you were two, how the hair in your pigtails would flop up and down to the rhythm of your unstable toddle. I remember when you were three how you would call a lake a "lape" and a river a "ribber." And then when you were four, how quickly you caught on to my sarcasm, would shake your head and say, "Mother, you're joking."

You have changed so much since that first morning you spent with us, a morning that altered my life so drastically that sometimes it still feels like I'm catching my breath. I imagine that I won't ever stop feeling this way, won't ever stop having a portion of my brain dedicated to the thought of where you are and what you're doing, won't ever be able to escape the constant, nagging hope that you are happy and fulfilled. My pulse is forever closer to the surface because of you, because of my responsibility toward you, and I can't thank you enough for the dimension that this has added to what it means to be alive.

Love,
Mama

ACKNOWLEDGMENTS

I would like to thank my editor, Jeremie Ruby-Strauss, who trusted in the contents of these letters before anyone else ever did. This book would not exist without his vision and hard work or those many phone calls where he had to convince me to trust them as much as he did.

Many thanks to my agent, Betsy Lerner, for sticking by my side through the roller-coaster sine curve of a blogger's psyche. No small feat.

Thanks to the readers of my website whose interest in these letters motivated me to keep writing them for as long as I did. One day my daughter will know how many strangers cared very deeply about her first steps.

And finally, all of my love and thanks to Leta Elise, whose story in these pages has touched so many lives, most importantly my own, because she taught me what it means to be human.

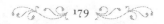

Printed in the United States
By Bookmasters